# Island

\\ˈī-lənd\\

*noun*

a tract of land surrounded by water and smaller than a continent

"we travelled to the island by boat"

Copyright © 2016

All rights reserved. No part of this publication may be reproduced, stored in a retrieval system or transmitted in any form by any means without the prior permission of the copyright owner. Enquiries should be made to the publisher.

Every effort has been made to ensure that this book is free from error or omissions. However, the Publisher, the Author, the Editor or their respective employees or agents, shall not accept responsibility for injury, loss or damage occasioned to any person acting or refraining from action as a result of material in this book whether or not such injury, loss or damage is in any way due to any negligent act or omission, breach of duty or default on the part of the Publisher, the Author, the Editor, or their respective employees or agents.

The Author, the Publisher, the Editor and their respective employees or agents do not accept any responsibility for the actions of any person - actions which are related in any way to information contained in this book.
The moral right of the author has been asserted.

National Library of Australia Cataloguing-in-Publication entry

Author: Doak, Amy

Title: Island Homes Of The World

ISBN: 9780994412669

Subject: Interior Decoration, Decoration Of Specific Rooms In Residential Buildings, Travel

Dewey Number: 747.7

Images by agreement with photographers. Please see page 126 for credits. The publisher has done its utmost to attribute the copyright holders of all the visual materials used. If you nevertheless think that a copyright has been infringed, please contact the publisher.

Published by:
Of The World Publishing
PO Box 8070
BENDIGO SOUTH LPO  VIC  3550

www.oftheworldbooks.com

# Island Homes
## of the world

# Contents

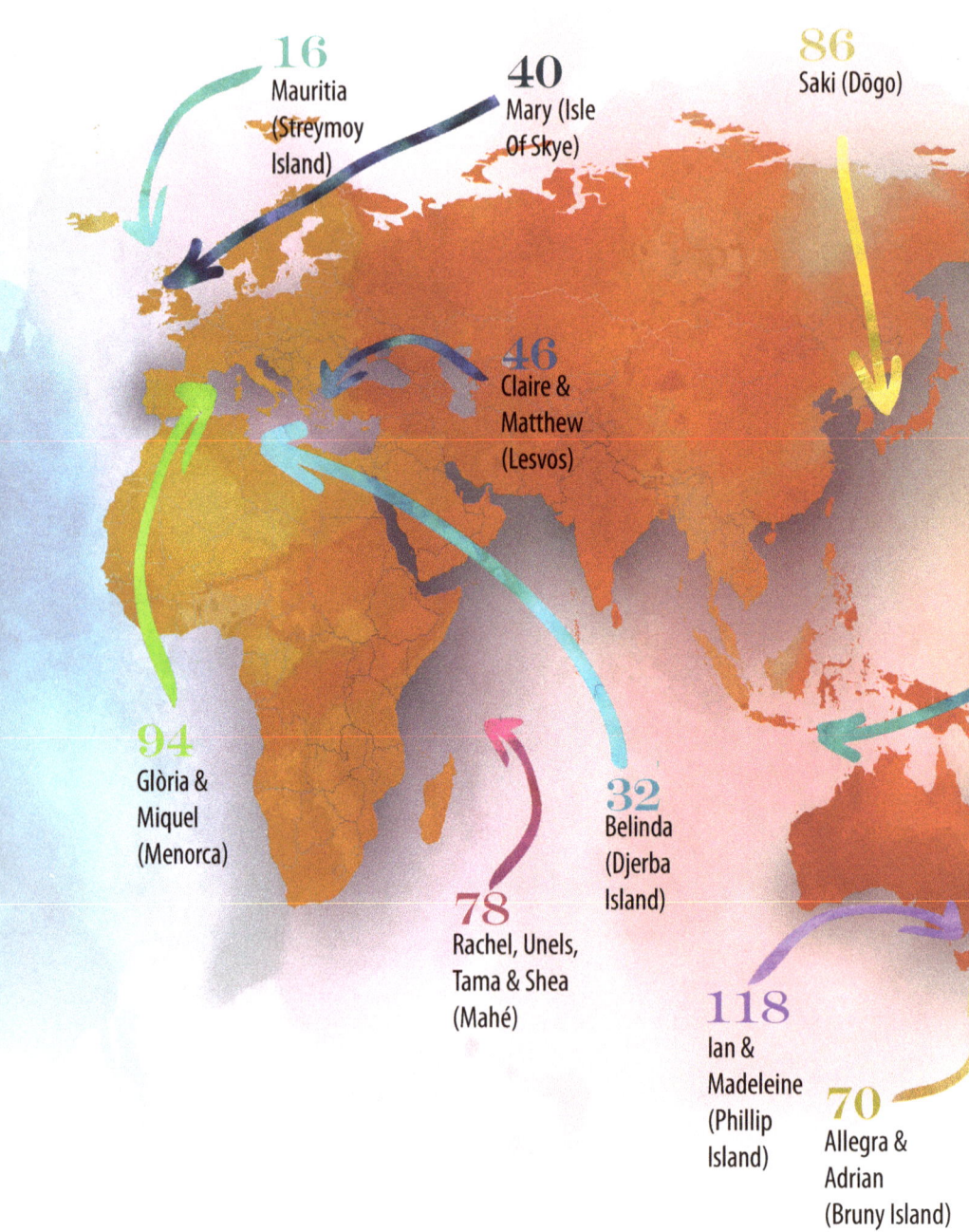

**16** Mauritia (Streymoy Island)

**40** Mary (Isle Of Skye)

**86** Saki (Dōgo)

**46** Claire & Matthew (Lesvos)

**94** Glòria & Miquel (Menorca)

**32** Belinda (Djerba Island)

**78** Rachel, Unels, Tama & Shea (Mahé)

**118** Ian & Madeleine (Phillip Island)

**70** Allegra & Adrian (Bruny Island)

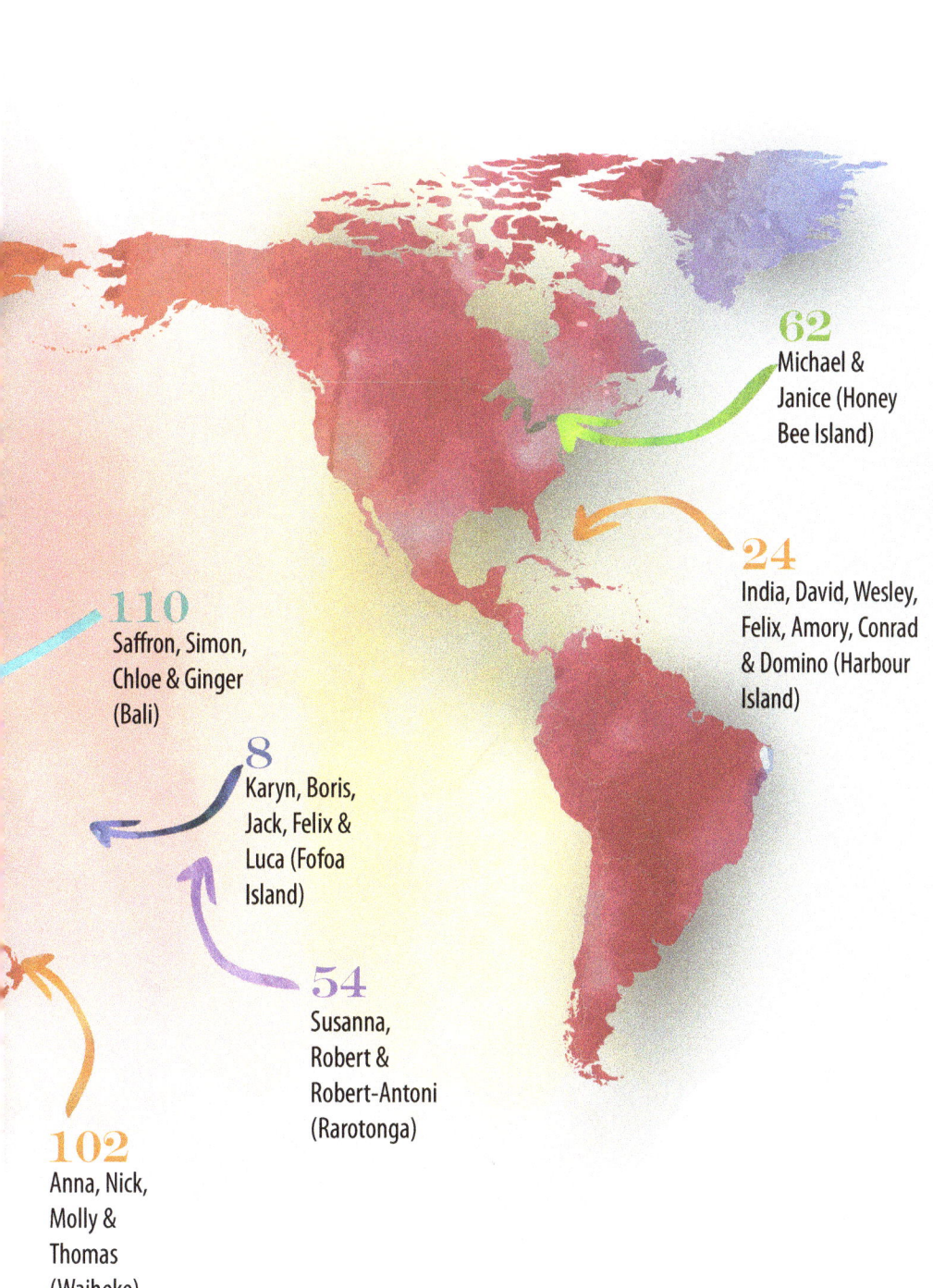

# Introduction

**There's something magical about an island.**

As the world gets smaller and busier, the appeal of escaping to a little, undiscovered corner is ever appealing. Over the years, our obsession with islands hasn't waned. From Shakespeare's *The Tempest* through to more modern-day classics such as *The Island of Dr Moreau, The Lord of The Flies* or even Alex Garland's *The Beach*, we continue to find a fascination with island life. TV offerings have entertained us with such shows as *Gilligan's Island, Magnum PI* and *Death In Paradise*, enjoying perfect weather, a laid-back lifestyle and just enough adventure to keep things interesting.

Fictional islands tend to be lost paradises where poetry and contemplation happen, or places where morality is tested or physical and psychological hardships are endured. In real life, the possibility of discovering a truly deserted island and making it your home is becoming less and less likely. However, as you will discover here, it's not completely impossible. Likewise, the challenges of loneliness and isolation are – thanks in part to the magic of the Internet and technology –not what they once may have been.

In 2009, Queensland Tourism launched a campaign for 'The Best Job In The World' that entailed looking after a group of islands in The Great Barrier Reef and living on Hamilton Island. Over 35,000 people from 200 countries applied for the position, proving that island life is certainly appealing.

In this book I've spoken to 15 people who have decided to make island life more than just a holiday or a whim. For them, it can be hard work, challenging and difficult but also beautiful, inspiring and exciting. Despite their protests that island life isn't always perfect, I am not convinced. It seems to me that each of these people have set out to create their perfect way of life and have achieved it in such a way that I am now tempted to seek out an island all of my very own. I hope, when you've finished reading, that you might be too.

# Fofoa, Tonga
## Karyn, Boris, Jack, Felix & Luca

Tonga is a Polynesian kingdom of more than 170 islands, many uninhabited, and most lined with white beaches and coral reefs and covered with tropical rainforest. Located just east of the International Date Line, it's often said that Tonga is 'the place where time begins', although many tourists will joke that, with the pace of local life, it's where time stands still.

Fifty-two of the Tongan islands are home to approximately 103,000 people and 70 per cent of Tongans reside on the main island of Tongatapu. Neiafu is the second largest town in Tonga with a population of about 6,000. It's an important centre for tourism with many yachts anchoring in the Port of Refuge.

Karyn and Boris had a passion for travel and far away places long before they even met…in fact, that's how they met! Back in 2000, Karyn left her information technology job in the UK to go travelling. She ended up in Zanzibar and met Boris who, originally from Germany, was running a hotel and restaurant. Seven years later the pair and eldest son, Jack, left Zanzibar for Nelson (New Zealand). With two more sons (Felix and Luca) arriving to complete the family, they then left Nelson for perhaps the biggest adventure of their lives.

"We wanted to live in an environment that was more closely connected to nature," Karyn explains about their move to Fofoa, a 100-acre island 12 miles across the sea from the Tongan town of Neiafu. "We wanted our children to have more of a 'wild' childhood…not fighting over screen time. Plus, we loved the idea of living somewhere warm and having an adventure!"

When the family first moved to Tonga, Karyn and the children stayed in Neiafu while Boris made the weekly journey to Fofoa to clear some of the eight acres of land they had leased. "Progress was painfully slow," Karyn admits. "Jack (the eldest) was not even six years old, and none of the boys could

swim with confidence, so bringing them to the island was a real mission in organisation. Several times we would get on the boat and want to head straight home again! I remember though, when Boris called me from Tonga and we had to make a choice then and there to sign the lease or not…I said 'well, we could live an ordinary life, or an extraordinary life.' In the beginning, that bit me on the bum more than a few times and we've had moments where it's felt like a long eight years, but I wouldn't change it for anything."

When the family did move to the island, they lived in tents for nine months while they built their first property – *Happy 'api*. 'Api means 'allotment' in Tongan. "*Happy 'api* is primarily constructed from coconut logs milled here on the island," Karyn says. "We believe that it's the only vertical log home in the world. The flooring in the kitchen is local wood from the island, felled and milled by Boris. The kitchen is made from cedar and incorporates branches from the moli (mandarin) trees, in recognition of the history of Fofoa, which once served as a mandarin plantation. The wood theme even continues to the sink, which is the heart of a cedar log. We literally designed the bathroom around a huge piece of coral rock and that is now a garden feature! Originally we wanted to construct a home entirely from materials sourced on the island, however time necessitated a compromise and we have had to import some materials as well."

*Happy 'api* is very, very open plan. "We only recently made doors for the rooms," Karyn laughs. "I probably only close the shutters and doors two or three times a year. This definitely contributes to an intimate, social space for our family. By primarily using natural materials in the house, we have created a very calm, nurturing environment with no real boundaries between the exterior and interior. It also means that we are always breathing in fresh, South Pacific sea air!

"After three years on the island, we knew we would need a business to make staying here viable so we decided to build *The Beach House* as a self-contained holiday home. The location is stunning – the deck spans across huge coral rocks with views across the lagoon to other South Pacific islands. We divide our time between the two houses depending on climate and business.

"*The Beach House* is made from coral rock both harvested here on the island and shipped in from town. The walls of the bathroom are lined with bamboo from a nearby island. The flooring in the bedroom was a last-minute experiment to parquet using the middle section of some coconut logs left

over from *Happy 'api*. Even the wardrobe is a piece of driftwood and the hangers are made from lathes of a coconut. Door handles are either clam or cowrie shells collected from the beach, and root wood is a perfect replacement for hooks."

The business of running *The Beach House* also includes year-round fishing charters (which Boris has won awards for) and whale watching tours during whale season – with Karyn as the guide and Boris as the skipper. Karyn also home schools the boys, although Jack has just this year decided to attend boarding school in New Zealand but comes home to the island every holidays. But don't think Karyn and Boris are relaxing in a hammock with a coconut and straw in their hands during their downtime. Between the businesses and the everyday tasks involved in simply surviving, island life is not always easy. "The pace of life is slower here, but it takes a lot of work to maintain a home and a business on the island. Plans change all the time – logistics is never a strong point living on an island – so you need to be flexible in your attitude and develop a lot of genuine patience.

"There are constant challenges living on a remote island. Sourcing food and provisioning dry goods that we don't have onsite involves a 45-minute boat trip through rough seas to get to town and you need to be extremely organised as items we require have to come from the US or New Zealand.

"As a consequence, we try to be as self-sufficient as possible, particularly in the garden. This year, we've increased the amount of chickens so that we don't have to rely on town for our eggs. Sometimes the solitude can get to you… a simple coffee with a friend always involves a boat ride and it can take all day. When we first moved here, our only form of communication was VHF radio. Originally, our telephone reception meant sitting in the middle of the lagoon to make a call. Now we have WiFi, so I can Skype, although this is limited as we have to bounce our signal from another island with its own power system. It has made a huge difference in being able to stay in touch with family and friends, even those who live in Tonga.

"Upkeep of buildings, boats and essential off-grid equipment is a constant challenge with the salty air, so regular maintenance is really important. We are also wholly reliant on rainwater so we need to ensure that it is pure and drinkable – and we need to be mindful of our consumption to get us through the dry season. It can be stressful relying on the elements. Cloudy days without wind or rain mean that we have to resort to our back-up generator."

Having lived in many countries over the years, Karyn and Boris couldn't imagine living anywhere else. "The overwhelming beauty of our location never fails to amaze me. Trips into town often bring sightings of turtles, dolphins or whales as well as the stunning islands. Simple details, like collecting eggs in the morning or picking kola (local lime) from a tree grown from seed brings me daily happiness. Seasonal changes – like spotting the first humpback whale arriving – is very exciting and realising that all the food on our plate was either caught, grown or raised locally is so rewarding."

"We have loved sharing our home with visitors and guests – their reaction to what we've created continues to feed our enthusiasm for our vision and brings us much needed contact with the outside world. Tonga is a beautiful country. The Tongan people are very welcoming and accepting of our strange palangi (white, or European) ways! It's a very peaceful place to live with a great deal of personal freedom and a safe environment for the children. "

The family still love to travel, but these days the few chances to do so tend to be trips back to Europe and the UK to see family. "It's a quick culture fix when we are back there – museums and a show – and it's important that the boys are accustomed to a different way of life and get used to large groups of people. It's overwhelming at first, even for Boris and I. Interestingly, since living on the island, cold countries really start to look appealing to visit. . . places that I'd never considered before, like Alaska and Finland. Stepping out of your comfort zone and seeing the world from another perspective is really what travel is all about. Although, I am not sure there is anywhere in the world better than our home."

*For more about Karyn, Boris and their beautiful island home, visit www.tongabeachhouse.com*

"The overwhelming beauty of our location never fails to amaze me. Trips into town bring sightings of turtles, dolphins or whales as well as the stunning islands."

# Streymoy, Faroe Islands
## Mauritia

Just a short flight from the UK, yet a lifetime away from the world, the magical Faroe Islands are an archipelago between the Norwegian Sea and the North Atlantic Ocean – approximately half way between Norway and Iceland and 320 kilometres north-northwest of Great Britain. With a population of just under 50,000, the islands are an autonomous country within the Danish Kingdom. A mix of the ancient and modern, you will find multicoloured cottages and grass-roofed wooden churches; tiny, once-inaccessible hamlets linked by a remarkable series of road-tunnels and breathtaking scenery in an unpredictable climate.

Streymoy is the largest and most populated island of the Faroe Islands and stretches 47 kilometres long and 10 kilometres wide. On the west coast of Streymoy, you will find the village of Kvívík – one of the oldest settlements in the Faroes. Excavations have shown the remains of Viking houses and the oldest house in the village was built in the 18th century. With the small river, Stora, and a narrow bay moving through the village, the region is perfect for the keen fisherman...or woman.

German writer, Mauritia, used to travel to the Faroe Islands regularly for fly-fishing and one day decided to buy herself a property there. Before she knew it, she was the owner of two homes! "The house next door to the home I bought was an ancient farm house and I was deeply impressed by its traditional beautiy," Mauritia says. "The former owners used it rarely – for family get-togethers, or having coffee and cake. They had invited me over a few times and when they decided to sell it, I think it gave them some comfort that I would be the new owner. They saw how well I took care of the neighbouring house and they could be sure I would respect their home."

Mauritia admits that her cultural inquisitiveness has influenced her personal and professional life. "I worked for 25 years with the German airline, Lufthansa, and that took me all over the world to

many exotic locations. I then worked for 10 years running a studio for the reproduction of historic clothing which took me deep in to European history. Fishing has fascinated me since I was a child though, both from a sporting and a biological perspective. I approach animals, nature and culture with the greatest respect and understanding. There is hardly a profession that furnishes one with so many stories as fishing – from the high seas to wispy rivulets, from rich to poor, from 'mate' to 'His Royal Majesty' and sadly, also from life to death. I have come to know them and have made it my task to tell their stories."

Having family and friends visit throughout the year keeps Mauritia busy, and she now also rents the farmhouse to tourists during the summer months. "Most of my guests are spending their holidays with walking tours in the magnificent landscape, but I am also welcoming many anglers who appreciate the incomparable pureness of fly fishing opportunities which the Faroe Islands offer.

"What I love most about the Faroe Islands are the wonderful people. They are honest, polite, down to earth and have an incredibly great kind of humour. The local women I have met are virtuosi in baking, making desserts and knitting. For centuries they have dealt with what little they had and made the best of it. The traditional food – all coming from the sea, the green hills and the air around – like fish, lamb and birds, is all delicious and matches the rough climate.

"The landscape here is one of the most beautiful I have seen. There are hundreds of shades of green in the mountains and hundreds of shades of blue in the sea. The air is incredibly clean and clear. All kinds of oranges in the sunset, the northern lights from September to April and on clear nights you can see the Milky Way. For me, as a fly fisher, there are fish everywhere! I can fish from the sea or the mountain lakes, which are only a stone's throw away. Here, no spot is further than five kilometres from the sea. In Germany, I grew up close to a river and I love to be surrounded by water. No wonder I love it here."

Mauritia's appreciation for culture and the local landscape has led her to create a home that is true to the local style both inside and out. "The most typical design element of traditional Faroese houses is definitely the grass roofs. They have many advantages: strong winds and storms cannot do any damage; they offer good insulation and you do not hear the rain hammering on the roof.

"Living in such a wet and windy archipelago, you need warm, cosy and dry homes. In older times, when they had no oil heating, they had to built their homes with the greatest care so that they are warm and cosy and dry with little effort. A cove in the centre; timber walls, ceilings and floors; low ceilings; benches, sheep fur and woollen clothes were basic elements to guarantee a fine home. Attached to every house is a 'drying shed', where still today meat and fish hang for drying."

In today's modern world, Mauritia believes there are definitely more advantages than disadvantages when it comes to living on an island. "Tranquility and relaxation are the huge values. You are only aware, every now and then, that you are living on an island, when the ship or plane hasn't arrived so the storage racks in the supermarket are lacking some item or another!

"I am not a lover of hot temperatures and I am thankful that I can flee these incredible heat waves we are suffering from due to global warming. I am very fond of Scandinavian countries. For me, they have found a perfect way for future challenges concerning society – education, environmental issues, politics and stability.

"Every minute that I stay on the Faroe Islands it simply amazes me. How these grass-covered mountains in the middle of the wild North Atlantic have managed to survive. I am deeply impressed by the skills of those living here. Especially during the last century. They are, on the other hand, also so incredibly relaxed."

All over the globe, people joke about 'island time' and despite the cooler climate, it appears that the Faroe Islands are no exception. "This is the land of 'maybe'. No stress, what we cannot do today, we can do tomorrow," laughs Mauritia. "All depends on the weather. It is always like this. Today, people are not so dependent on the weather conditions but the attitude is still the same. It's quite different sometimes in Germany. It's nice taking things a bit easier.

"While working for the airline, I have travelled the globe and visited almost every place you could imagine. I ended up here and this was my decision. I wouldn't wish to be anywhere else in the world. I love Europe, European values and culture. This is the place for me to be.

"Of course, if I were to take a holiday…perhaps I could imagine Alaska or the west of Canada. Then, without a doubt, it would only be somewhere that I could fish!"

*To discover more about fly fishing and to stay at the farmhouse in the Faroe Islands, go to www.flyfishing.fo and Mauritia's book 'The Faroe Islands, The Last Paradise, A Travel Guide For Sport Fisher' is available at www.bokhandil.fo*

*"There is hardly a profession that furnishes one with so many stories as fishing – from the high seas to the wispy rivulets, from rich to poor and, sadly, from life to death. I have come to know them & made it my task to tell their stories."*

# Harbour Island, Bahamas

## India, David, Wesley, Felix, Amory, Conrad & Domino

Sitting southeast of Florida and just north of Cuba in the Atlantic Ocean, the Bahamas is a coral-based archipelago comprising of 700 islands and 2,400 cays. From the uninhabited to the resort-packed, the Bahamas relies heavily on tourism for its economic activity. Of course, with its blue-green waters, sandy beaches and fabulous reputation as an island paradise (three James Bond movies have been filmed there) the Bahamas is on many people's bucket list. The Bahamas served as a British Colony from 1718 until becoming an independent Commonwealth realm in 1973 meaning over the years it's become popular with Brits and English-speaking tourists.

One of the prettiest islands in the group is Harbour Island. Famous for its pink sand beaches, the little island (less than five kilometres from top to bottom) is known as Briland to the locals. With colourful English Colonial-style buildings, flower-lined streets, humble pastel cottages and sleek French bistros, Harbour Island's population of just 2,000 offers a quirky mix of fisherman through to millionaires – waving hello as they pass each other on the streets driving identical golf carts!

Before settling in Harbour Island, British-born India had travelled the world working as a model and photographer. Taking a little respite from her busy life, India ended up in the Bahamas and found herself in Harbour Island. David, an old friend, was running a small hotel there. Four months later, the two were madly in love and India was pregnant. "Living on a small tropical island in the middle of an ocean sounds hugely romantic but, in reality, being strangers in a strange land and raising five children can be quite challenging," India admits. "However, with a shared sense of humour and a great deal of patience, this life brings us much adventure.

"Finding myself unexpectedly barefoot and pregnant, David and I wanted a house that we could make into a home. *Hibiscus Hill* was set back from the beach, which I liked as it felt a little more

private, sitting amongst a grove of coconut trees."

India and David bought *Hibiscus Hill* virtually unseen. The estate agent wouldn't let the couple inside the house but, with India peering through the windows and David touring the gardens, they both agreed that this was the place for them. "There were no preconceived ideas of how life should be lived here. There were few other foreign families living full time on the island then, so we felt a little like pioneers in some respect," India explains. "I loved that, and obviously the fact that there were no parking tickets, no rush hour traffic, incredibly clear night skies and a pink sandy beach at the bottom of our garden."

*Hibiscus Hill* was built in the 1950s but the couple set about making changes to have it appear as though it had been there since the 1850s. India says the architecture and the view from the harbour have hardly changed in 200 years and she was keen to create that same timeless aesthetic in her own home. When it came to design and décor, much of India's style is organic and yet also very much 'India'. Growing up with a designer father, becoming an adult in the fashion and style world and also being influenced by her new surroundings resulted in a relaxed yet very elegant family home. Making use of natural materials and fairly muted tones means that the odd pop of colour really shines – much like the beautiful flowers on the island – and the combination of family history, international lives, classic British taste and the traditions of the Caribbean are all apparent. "Because of the tropical weather we are able to have all of our doors and windows wide open – we aren't fans of air conditioning – and it's a very inside-out lifestyle. We also like to bring the outside in and have oversized vases filled with palm fronds everywhere. They add drama and certainly shout island life."

India says life on the island has, without question, been an adventure. "Living on a small island in the Bahamas has certainly provided us with quite a colourful backdrop to raise our kids," she laughs. "There is absolute freedom for them to roam anywhere safely. They've developed vivid imaginations and all were taught to wield a machete at a young age!

"The Bahamas certainly comes with an imagined idea of life: lazy afternoons swaying under palm fronds, on pink sand beaches, as Ursula Andress wanders out of a turquoise coloured ocean… Of course there are palm trees, pink sands and turquoise waters but there are some challenges too: like a three-month hurricane season; a doctor that services three islands so can't always be found in an emergency; no dentist, vet or obgyn and I when I gave birth to four of my five children, I had to time it carefully as a boat or plane was involved! We lose power about three times a week for several hours a day and when the freight boat can't get in, the grocery store stands empty."

Getting to Harbour Island isn't an easy process either. A flight into North Eleuthera from Miami, Nassau or Fort Lauderdale then requires a water taxi to Harbour Island. For India, who travels a great deal for work, this means that although life has its moments of stress and arduous logistics, it also has allowed Harbour Island to become a true haven. "My life is presently rather consumed with building a direct sales business (www.indiahicks.com) which is terrifying and exciting all at the same time," India says. "Life outside the home involves lots of travel and hideous airport security. When I am at home, I get to take my children to school on a golf cart, when the only bit of traffic that we might encounter is a chicken crossing the road. It's quite a different pace of life to the one I lead when I am travelling for work."

With the chaos of the business world, and India constantly being on the move, it's hard to imagine that she misses anything about the rest of the world when she's back on Harbour Island – even with the chance of hurricanes and power outages! However, it seems even in paradise, there is something to yearn for. "I love being somewhere with lots of gigantic movie theatres. I must admit, I do miss the movies."

*See more of India's lifestyle brand and story at www.indiahicks.com and check out her latest beautiful book* India Hicks Island Style *at bookstores and online.*

*"Living on a small island in the Bahamas has certainly provided us with quite a colourful backdrop to raise our kids. There is absolute freedom for them to roam safely."*

# Djerba Island, Tunisia
## Belinda

Though relatively small in size, Tunisia, the northernmost country in Africa, offers great diversity both geographically and demographically (having been invaded by Arabs, Normans, Ottomans and the French over the last century and a half). To the north of the country, in the Gulf of Gabes, lies the island of Djerba. With a population of just over 158,000 the island is known as a tourist mecca with beautiful coastlines and fabulous markets. It's also famous for being the backdrop of the first *Star Wars* film.

Beyond the busy beaches, Djerba's main appeal lies in its ancient architecture and strong, historic identity as a fortress island. Just 7km inland from Houmd Souk (the largest town on the island) sits the village of Erriadh. With its historic Medina's labyrinth of narrow passageways, bougainvillea-filled courtyards and hidden alcoves, the village is a step back in time. Goats roam freely, locals dress in traditional tunics and donkey carts clatter along dusty roads. Despite Tunisia's recent political upheavals with the Revolution and historic cultural battles throughout northern Africa over the centuries, in Djerba Muslims and Jews live peacefully side-by-side.

Dutch-born Belinda is definitely a resident of the world. With three daughters spread across the globe, Belinda spent 30 years living in Canada. Work took her back to Europe and she was restoring old farmhouses in Italy when she first discovered Djerba Island and northern Africa. "My partner was Italian but he loved Tunisia and was keen to do a project there," Belinda explains. "He wanted to construct a new home though and my passion is restoration so that didn't interest me. When I stumbled upon this beautiful old village – Erriadh – I fell in love."

Ten years on and Belinda has now restored four old homes (or houches, as they are known) in the village, the first of which was a tumbledown ruin. "It was completely destroyed and no one was living in it. The second home I purchased was the property next door and at the time a local family was

living there. They led a simple life and the house reflected that – there was even a cow living in one of the rooms."

The languages spoken in Djerba are predominantly Arabic and French and Belinda drew upon her high school French skills to get started on the restoration with local trades. "I speak enough French to get by," she laughs. "I love a challenge though. If I know what to expect, life becomes predictable. I like things to be a little alien."

Belinda admits that culturally, and physically, there were some challenges setting up home in Djerba…starting with temperatures of up to 48 degrees celcius in the summer. "The heat is an issue, but one that residents have been dealing with for thousands of years. Locals start early in the morning and then stop at noon for around four hours when it gets too hot. They do everything in the shade. I'm not a person who lays in the sun. We have Parisians come and stay and they just want to lay in the sun! I say, 'are you crazy?'

"You also have to deal with calls to prayer and religious holidays. It's better not to work at this time – or not to expect work to be done – because you will drive yourself insane. Coming here, I definitely underestimated what it would be like to be a woman working in an Arab world. Perhaps the biggest hurdle is, when you first arrive, you think everyone is just like you. They dress Western, mimic a lot of Western behaviour and there are some fast food places and Western music. But my first visit here was before the Revolution and, in a way, that time was easier. There was a sense of order. People were more fearful, but a little more respectful too. You can't take anything at face value here – even more so since the Revolution. There is a lot of corruption and I didn't understand that – even after my time in Italy, which was an eye-opener in itself. They want a democracy and they should have it… but, in a way, they don't know what democracy is. They think it is doing what you please.

"In the beginning, I had a lot of Europeans, particularly French people, come and visit. But, with the political climate changing over the past few years you don't see as many Westerners in this part of the world. Tourism has always been the primary industry here but last summer I saw very few white people around the island."

Despite the political issues, Belinda says that there is a great deal to love and appreciate about the country. "There used to be a lot of Jewish families here, especially back in the 1960s. There is

a Jewish medina and Erriadh is also home to the oldest synagogue in Africa so it's an important pilgrimage for many Jewish people – particularly African Jews. Muslims and Jews have lived side-by-side in peace for many years on Djerba. Culturally, it's a fascinating place."

When it came to renovating her home, Belinda did a lot of research and learnt all she could about the region. "I have trekked a lot of Tunisia and I have great respect for the culture and the history. Over the years I have dealt with a lot of buildings of historical significance and it's very important for me to do things right. I have a lot of respect for old buildings and you must treat them with the dignity they deserve. Because the first home was so run down, I sourced a lot of materials from other places and the challenge was combining the old with the new.

"I have a creative background and I was really able to indulge myself with this project. I visited local artisans to have special items made – right down to having a say in how my rugs were to be woven. I have learnt so much. They have a process of dealing with the heat and helping insulate the houses here – the art of tadelakt. It is mixing up plaster, calcium and sand with a coloured pigment and then letting that sit and brew before applying layers on the wall and sealing it with a kind of wax. I just love that."

Belinda didn't renovate the homes for tourism – that came later. "I enjoyed doing it just for me. I wanted it to be beautiful and comfortable for me to live in, and a place that my family would enjoy visiting. They are not very big homes, so every bit of space is important and has a function. In the outside courtyard I have a plunge pool – again, it's small to make the best of the space, but very deep to ensure you can completely immerse yourself in the cool water on a very hot day. Even though we are only seven kilometres from the sea, it's still a distance so it's nice to have water at your door. Each room has its own bathroom. A good fridge is a priority. It's also important to be able to keep the space clean – the heat and the wind means it can get dusty and dirty quickly and that makes you feel hot and uncomfortable. Disposing of garbage easily is also something that makes life better, although that is getting easier. When I first moved here, a donkey and cart used to come by and collect the rubbish. Now we have big bins.

"It's a real experience staying in the village. Everyone who has stayed tells me that it exceeds their expectations. A lot of the tourist places are beautiful, with their five-star luxury and inclusions, but it's a special experience being in the centre of a small community like this. The local women in colourful dresses and headscarves are busy in the street during the day, the market is buzzing on Sunday morning and at night you have a quiet, big sky filled with stars. You feel like you are going back in time.

"If I were to ever leave Djerba, I would really miss my homes. They are very organic – part cave-dwelling almost - and also very historical. I don't think I would find somewhere like this anywhere else in the world. The whole feel of the place, really."

For now though, Belinda continues to travel, share her homes and enjoy all that the world has to offer. "My motto in life is 'just do it'. If you have the opportunity, do it. You can always go back to what you're used to. There's so much to learn though, and so many interesting people to meet. It's so worth stepping out of the box."

*If you would love the have the opportunity to stay in one of Belinda's beautiful homes in Erriadh, visit www.safran-djerba.com*

"It's a special experience being in the centre of a small community like this. The local women in colourful dresses and headscarves, the buzzing Sunday market and the quiet, star-filled nights... you feel like you are back in time."

# Isle of Skye, Scotland
## Mary

Scotland is part of the United Kingdom and covers the northern third of Great Britain. It shares a border with England to the south, and is otherwise surrounded by the Atlantic Ocean with the North Sea to the east the North Channel and Irish Sea to the south-west. In addition to the mainland, Scotland is made up of more than 790 islands, including the Northern Isles and the Hebrides. The Hebrides are two island chains – the Inner Hebrides off the west coast of mainland Scotland, and the Outer Hebrides to the south east.

The Inner Hebrides comprises of 35 inhabited and 44 uninhabited islands. The largest and most northernly island in the Inner Hebrides is Skye, or the Isle of Skye. Occupied since the Mesolithic period, the island's history includes a time of Norse rule and a long period of domination by Clan Macleod and Clan Donald. Its name comes from the old Norse 'sky-a', meaning 'cloud island' which is a Viking reference to the mist-shrouded Cuillin Hills. The popular tourist destination offers a stunning landscape of velvet moors, jagged mountains, towering sea cliffs and sparkling lochs. With plenty of castles, museums, art galleries and cosy pubs and restaurants, Skye has lots to enjoy. The main town of Portree, with its pretty and colourful pastel houses on the bay, is the largest settlement with a population of just under 2,500. Towards the south of Skye, is the Sleat Penninsula. Referred to as 'the garden of Skye', Sleat provides a grandstand for magnificent scenery such as stunning views of the Isle of Rhum.

Taking advantage of the beautiful vistas that Sleat has to offer is local architect, Mary, who set out to design and build her home in 2008. The seemingly simple house hides many clever features that ensure it is perfect year-round. "It is an unusual building for Skye," Mary admits of what is known as '*The Shed.*' "The materials are taken from agricultural buildings – corrugated steel, sheet frame and larch cladding."

The simple design was inspired by the traditional barns and sheds spotted throughout Scotland and the Hebrides and although the corrugated and larch cladding provides the look of a 'shed', the features that can't be seen provide a practical, modern and economical way to live. The house has Scotland's first grant-aided exhaust-air heat pump which, along with solar panels, powers the under-floor heating and the hot-water system. External shutters can be slid into place on a track in front of the large window which offers protection during the wild Highland winter storms. In addition to the under-floor heating the home is also over-insulated. There is a large wood burning stove which provides a point of focus in the open plan living space (as well as additional warmth!) The house also has its own water supply and an outdoor shower.

Mary has furnished the home in a simple, almost Scandinavian style – which is fitting really, given the home's northern European setting. With timber furniture, oak joinery, white floor-to-ceiling bookcases and slate-grey tiles, the house doesn't try to compete with the beauty of its natural surroundings. Soft furnishings echoing the colour of Scottish heather with sage-green and dusty-pinks ensure a relaxed and simple feeling of space throughout.

What really makes the house special though, is the magnificent views from every angle. Mary says that the siting and layout of The Shed was key to make best use of the location. Upstairs, a cantilevered picture window offers a view of the Cuillin mountain range, while the large glazing downstairs faces south-west to the sea loch and across to the islands of Rhum and Canna.

"I do love the views...they are fantastic," Mary admits. "Certainly the design of the house was all about capturing them. But, I think I love the good times that I've had here with my friends and family so much more. I live alone, but have lots of friends and family who visit on a regular basis so there is always someone here to enjoy it with me." With four bedrooms, three bathrooms and two living spaces, there is more than enough room to share.

Mary loves spending time outdoors and thinks that she is definitely in the best part of the world

to appreciate nature. "Scotland is the most beautiful country that I've ever seen. As someone who cycles, climbs mountains and loves to sea kayak, it is the perfect place for me."

Despite the temptation to hunker down by the fire with the shutters closed during the blustery winters, Mary takes a more creative approach and rents her home out to others. "The main challenge of living in Skye, for me, is winter," she laughs. "It's wet and windy mostly! I travel a lot – I tend to escape to warmer climates in January – India, Costa Rica, Thailand and Vietnam. One day I hope to get to Australia and New Zealand."

With so much beauty surrounding her, despite the odd winter escape, Mary thinks it's hard to imagine wanting to be anywhere else.

*You can discover more about Skye and* The Shed *by visiting Mary's website: www.skyeshed.com*

"Scotland is the most beautiful country that I've ever seen. As someone who cycles, climbs mountains and loves to sea kayak, it is the perfect place for me."

# Lesvos, Greece
## Claire & Matthew

Located in southeastern Europe and with a population of around 10.8 million, Greece has one of the longest histories of any country in the world. It is considered the cradle of Western civilization and the birthplace of democracy, Western philosophy, the Olympic Games, Western literature, political science and major scientific and mathematical principles. Greece suffered greatly from the recession in the late 2000s and this triggered the Greek government-debt crisis – also known as the Greek depression – in 2009.

Despite its political and financial troubles, Greece remains an attractive and magical destination, filled with history. Greece has a large number of islands (some estimate up to 6,000) with just over 200 of them currently inhabited. The third largest island (after Crete and Euboea) is Lesvos (or Lesbos, as it's also known). With around 86,000 residents living on the 1,632 square kilometre island, the majority of people can be found in the island's capital, Mytilene. You will find old stone houses dotted around the island overlooking the sea, small villages, winding lanes, desert-like plains or dense olive groves (there are around 11 million olive trees on the island). With a cultural legacy stretching back to seventh-century-BC, there is no shortage of beauty or history on this exceptionally sunny island in the Aegean Sea.

Author, photographer and film maker, Claire, and her artist partner, Matthew, share their digs with their current batch of fur-children: rescue cats, Sweetie and Bingo, and rescue dogs, Nellie, Bertie, Tilley and Trixie. "We always have transient furry friends who pass through on their way to new families," Claire laughs. "We act as a foster home for them to be rehabilitated and loved."

For Claire and Matthew, creating a home in the Greek Islands was almost accidental. "It was not a conscious decision to make a village in Lesvos our home," Claire explains. "I decided to come here after my homeopath and friend, Victoria, suggested it might be a remedy after I told her I felt I'd lost my

creativity and didn't feel grounded. She was right. I took a trip to the island and immediately fell in love with the place. I felt instantly connected and started looking for a house. Once I found the house and Matthew and I made it our holiday home, it didn't take long for us to realise that we wanted to stay here longer and longer. So, we swapped our busy lives in London for a slower pace in a little Greek village."

As a creative person who has lived and worked all over the globe, Claire says that sees the beauty in any part of the world, however Lesvos has certainly captured her heart. "There are many things I love about Lesvos. I love the rugged landscape and the enormous skies. I love seeing the sea and swimming in the Aegean. I love living in a village community and the slow pace of life. I love the way I have time to witness the change of seasons and to be more aware of my surroundings. After living in London for 25 years, I now realise I missed nature and understand how much I need it in my life on a daily basis.

"I think all countries have positive and negative aspects and they also all have stereotypes. That's just what the world is like. For me, I don't just love one country. I think I could live in many countries around the world and I would find fabulous things about each one of them. I spend quite a lot of time in Australia and I love it there – just in a different way. I would be pretty happy in most places but I do need light, sunshine and warmth for me to stay for any length of time."

Despite its beauty, Greece and its islands have certainly faced a number of challenges over the last decade and Claire says that watching the changes has, at times, been heartbreaking. "There will be challenges anywhere you live and the biggest here for me has been the Greek crisis, which we have watched affect everyone over the last 10 years. Now we have the refugee crisis with thousands of refugees arriving in Greece every day. We have had the highest number of arrivals on this island and the island is ill equipped to deal with it. It's horrendous seeing these poor people arriving, fleeing from their homes and being separated from their loved ones. Walking with just a very small bag and their children. It's one thing to see it on TV but to be face-to-face with it is very confrontational. It's hard to know how to help or what to do. Matthew and I will sometimes pick up a carload and take them where they need to go, they are always grateful for any help. It makes me realise how fortunate I am to come back to my home and it definitely makes me really want to enjoy all that I have in my life."

This gratitude and love of simple things mean that Claire and Matthew enjoy a beautiful life on the island. "We have the rescue dogs, which I walk down the track each morning. Sometimes we walk all the way to the sea. I have Greek lessons although I'm not serious enough to be any good. I still persist though. I photograph and document life on the island. I swim and entertain friends. We seem to have a constant stream of guests and we enjoy showing them our favourite places on the island. And, of course, there is food. The food here is delicious and we enjoy eating seasonally. I just generally enjoy the days, which fly by."

The couple's little house is filled with light and just a touch of colour and Claire, who is a self-confessed minimalist, has found that over time the cottage has taken on a life of its own. "I would say I use similar design principles in every home I make but here the house is a village house so it's quite rustic," Claire says. "That means every element has a little bit of a rustic feel. In fact, Matthew has made most things in our home. Matthew failed at woodwork in school but has excelled in making our home beautiful. He has found a lot of things too, which have been lovingly restored and included. The result of this is that the house is not as minimal as we usually have a home and it is much more organic.

"The décor in our home is quite simple. Simple to me is the key to everything in life. All of my homes over the years have been painted white from top to toe so that light is reflected from every surface. Some people would fear snow blindness! The other thing, which is incredibly important to me, is light. I can never have enough light. Light pours in throughout the day here and this uplifts my spirit beyond anything."

Living in such a magical place, it's hard to imagine that Claire would ever want to leave. However, family, friends, work and a passion for travel means that the pull for new places will always be there. "I am always imagining living in other places. There are so many! I'm Australian and I love going back to Sydney and spending summer there. Effectively, I have two summers a year. I would love to live in Rome, I would love to live in Paris, I would love to live in Thailand or Japan, New York or India… or even another Greek Island!

"I adore travel, although we are limited because of the animals. This summer I went to Mykonos for a holiday. From one Greek island to another! I must admit, I do feel a little like I am on holiday most of the time. I have planned a holiday soon on an island off Thailand where I will be doing yoga and I cannot wait!"

*You can find out more about Claire by visiting her websites www.clairelloyd.com and www.clairelloydloves.com and her book,* My Greek Island Home, *where you can learn more about life on Lesvos, is available to purchase now.*

"We have the rescue dogs, which I walk down the track each morning. Sometimes we walk all the way to the sea. I have Greek lessons although I'm not serious enough to be any good.
I still persist though."

# Rarotonga, Cook Islands
## Susanna, Robert & Robert-Antoni

The Cook Islands is a nation of 15 islands in the central South Pacific Ocean. Rarotonga is the largest island and home to the majority of The Cook Islands' population (over 10,000 of the entire country's population of almost 15,000 live here). A 32 kilometre, round-the-island road links the beaches, coastal lagoons and reefs that make the area so popular for scuba divers and snorkelers and inland you will find a combination of volcanic peaks, ridges and dense rainforest.

The history of The Cook Islands dates back to the great Polynesian migration around 1500BC however archeologists have found evidence of human life as far back as 5000 years. Rarotonga was one of the last of The Cook Islands to be visited by European ships and quickly became a favourite of sailors and merchants. Many consider it to be the most beautiful island in the Pacific. Unlike Hawaii, Fiji or Tahiti, Rarotonga is still relatively untouched by commercialism and the relaxed nature of the island and its people is of great appeal to visiting tourists.

About one kilometre before you hit the busy (as busy as Rarotonga can get, at least!) tourist area of Muri, you will find a stunning two-bedroom timber property that overlooks Avana harbor and lagoon. The eco-friendly home was built using locally-sourced timbers milled specifically for the build. Susanna, her husband, Robert, and son, Robert-Antoni, call this property, '*Kaivera*', home. As well as renting out their beautiful house to lucky travellers, the family also runs a family farm business called ORGANICS Cook Islands.

Robert, who is a fourth generation grower, spent his younger years studying agriculture in Australia and then Spain and with his newly-found knowledge, combined with the family history of traditional agriculture, set about establishing a branch of eco-friendly fruit and vegetable cultivation in 1993.

Susanna, meanwhile, studied gardening and worked as a secretary for a large landscape engineering department in her native Spain in the early 1980s, however it was marketing that appealed to her. Soon she was working in media, then editorial for fashion magazines in Barcelona.

"I've always loved to travel," Susanna explains. "I've especially always been attracted to tropical islands. Since I can remember my eyes would get caught by the Pacific Islands whenever I had a map in my hands."

As Susanna approached her 40s, she decided to live her dream and take a year sabbatical to discover Polynesia. "I had travelled a lot before then, and been to many countries – the Caribbean Islands, Seychelles, Nauru, Australia, Fiji, Kiribati, the Mediterranean islands and other countries throughout the Middle East, Europe, Africa and the Americas."

Whilst enjoying her adventure, Susanna not only fell in love with The Cook Islands…but Robert as well! "After we were married, we moved back to Barcelona and lived there for three years. Our son was born there and my sisters live in Spain as well and we are very close. However, when Robert-Antoni was one year old, we decided to come back to Raro. I spend a lot of time on Skype now!"

Fast-forward almost 10 years, Robert and Susanna now supply organic culinary herbs, vegetables and fruit to more than 30 restaurants, hotels and families on the island. "It hasn't been easy for Robert to be an organic farming pioneer in Rarotonga but we love what we do."

Susanna admits that life on Rarotonga can sometimes be just as idyllic as one might imagine. "My son speaks mainly English but also understands and speaks basic Spanish, Catalan and Cook Islands Maori. He loves living here – he goes out fishing and catches crabs and regularly sees sea turtles, octopus, whales, giant trevally and coloured reef fish. They are all literally at our back door.

"After living in a city, where everything is cement, I really wanted a warm and comfortable timber home. I managed to get something even better though! The nobel timber we used to build the house was grown locally but originally would have come from my country (Spain) many years ago. The timber is all chemical-free and treated by us with oils and wax – Robert and I love nature and try to live in the most natural environment possible. Our little organic farm is home to many fruit trees and herbs – mountain apple, figs, star fruit, lemons, limes, oranges, papayas, bananas, oregano, parsley, rosemary, thyme, coriander, kale, chives, aloe vera, tomatoes... and we have just finished building a little chicken house so we will have free and fresh eggs!"

"There is no such thing as paradise though, even a place as beautiful as Raro has its downsides. Mosquitoes for one!" Susanna laughs. "We also get lots of rain, wind and mud and living this way means there is plenty of physical work to be done — looking after the land means there is a lot more work to do around the house compared to an apartment in the city... so nothing is perfect."

Susanna also notes that there is sometimes a clash of cultures. "The Cook Islands is essentially a Christian country and it's also a country that is not as developed as some others. Many locals are quite superstitious and religion is very powerful in the local community."

Susanna may not be superstitious, but she is very spiritual and it was important to her to have a home that was at one with nature. It was for this reason that the family made heavy use of timber throughout the home, and also employed the principles of Feng Shui.

"I chose timber for the windows, doors, shelves, floors, ceilings, tables, kitchen benches... even the shower frames! Wood is not only lovely to the touch, but it is also warm for your eyes. It's natural and isolable for electronic waves and low or high temperatures.

"I also wanted to ensure there was plenty of light. The shower is a double with a clear roof that opens to the stars and doors that open to the sun and the balcony — we hope to eventually have plenty of plants in this space some day. I find normal closed showers very claustrophobic so I wanted a shower that allowed you to feel free and fresh. Likewise, the kitchen opens right up with big doors and windows to the decking. We have no cabinet doors as I cook a lot and find doors disturbing. I can see the mountains to the west, beach views to the south and people can talk to me from the lounge or the deck when I am cooking."

Robert and Susanna's bedroom is on the third level of the home and opens to the harbor. "The view is so beautiful," Susanna says. "I can see from the ocean to the interior of the lagoon. Our head is at the north while sleeping — my son's is at the east (good for their personal feng shui) and every element of the home's design has a reason... a because."

Susanna credits coming from Barcelona with her passion for design. "Catalan people from Barcelona have grown up knowing about the importance of architecture — not just Antoni Gaudi! Barcelona has a rich history of the arts and, certainly for people in my generation, and those before me, design and architecture is important. I didn't want a flashy home; I wanted the opposite in fact. A home that was rustic and warm and allowed me to live my way — I never wanted to impress anyone."

With a dream home to work from each day, Susanna and her family have no plans to leave Rarotonga any time soon, but they are always open to new opportunities and further travel. "You never know! Australia... Chile... Marquise Islands... the South of Spain... there are many beautiful places in the world. To be honest though, I used to love traveling but now I find it a little uncomfortable. I love being at home. Although, I would like to buy fabrics in India, pots in Morocco, sail down the Nile in Egypt, eat a fresh salad in Greece, drink wine in the south of Italy, sleep under the sequoias in the USA, talk to the Galapagos in the Galapagos Islands... there are so, so many gorgeous places and tastes in our beautiful world!"

*You can visit Susanna's beautiful Cook Islands home. Go to www.kairevabeachhouse.com to learn more about the home, farm and organic life in Rarotonga.*

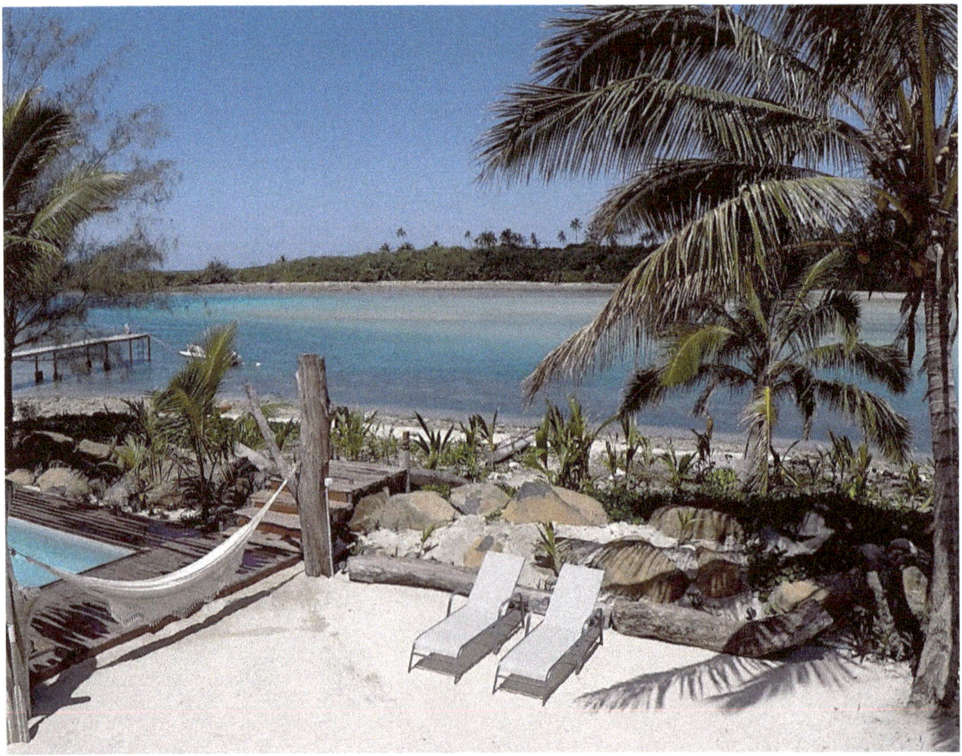

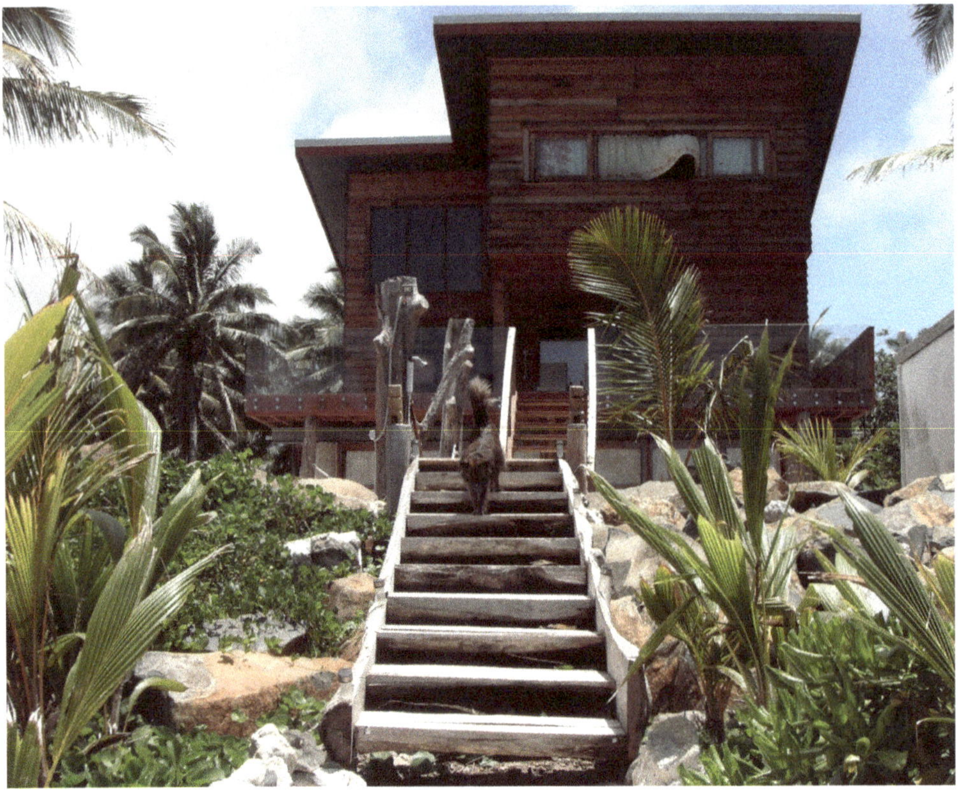

"After living in a city, where everything is cement, I really wanted a warm and comfortable timber home. I managed to get something even better though!"

# Honey Bee Island, Canada
## Michael & Janice

The Thousand Islands are an archipelago of 1,864 islands that sit on the US-Canada border in the Saint Lawrence River as it emerges from the northeast corner of Lake Ontario. They stretch for about 80km (50 miles) downstream and while the Canadian islands belong to the state of Ontario, the US islands belong to the state of New York. The many islands range in size from over 100 kilometres square (40 square miles) to smaller private islands, such as Honey Bee, which are occupied by a single residence. There are also some islands that are uninhabited outcroppings of rocks home to migrating waterfowl. To count as one of the Thousand Islands, the emergent land must be above water level year round and support at least two living trees.

Those living on or visiting the islands make use of the fresh water on their doorstep (or dock, as the case may be!) with boating, kayaking, fishing and swimming. The islands are a UNESCO biosphere site and a naturalist's paradise.

Honey Bee Island is home to Michael and Janice for at least four months of the year. They spend the full summer and early autumn in their island paradise. The retired couple live at their home in central California through late autumn and early winter and then spend late winter and spring at their villa on the French Riviera. Michael, who once had a career in law enforcement, and Janice, who worked as a dental hygienist, had talked about island living once on a holiday to Nova Scotia in Canada. At the time, they discounted it, due to the logistics of living on an ocean island.

"We didn't think anyone would come and visit us if we were too far away," Michael admits. In 2000, the couple took a trip to the East Coast of America for a family reunion and made room for a visit to Boldt Castle (on Heart Island in the Thousand Islands). "I'd torn a page from an inflight magazine three years earlier advertising the castle. It seemed like such a magical place to visit. After taking a cruise through the islands as part of the castle tour, Janice was thumbing through a real estate flier and said, 'hey, do you want to buy an island?'

"We set off the next morning with a realtor to have a look around. The trip through the Rift

between Hill and Wellesley Islands was stunningly beautiful, like riding the Jungle Cruise at Disneyland. We tried to play it cool, but we were so excited we could barely stand it. When we turned the corner of Godfrey Island we saw this absolute jewel. We'd barely entered the cabin and the deal was done."

Honey Bee Island is the size of a large city lot with a hand-adzed log cabin in its centre. Later owners added a porch, kitchen and second floor. Originally built as a fishing cabin, it has seen several lives before its current one – including being used as a speak easy during prohibition and the location of some fairly questionable parties following WWII.

"It had been vacant for two decades when we looked through it," Michael explains. "The listing agent was appalled to show us the property actually. The roof leaked, the exterior was overgrown with all manner of fallen branches and beavers had taken down a tree or two. The interior was furnished with rusting metal bedframes complete with mouse nests in the mattresses, there were squirrels living in the walls and the kitchen still had food in the pans on the stove. I thought that was perfect – it would definitely help with negotiations! A lot of people may have wanted to tear down the cabin but we saw it as a blank canvas waiting for us to paint our masterpiece."

It took 18 months just to get power to the island so it was the summer of 2002 before serious renovation work took place. It took a month for Michael and Janice to gut the property – filling over 100 large construction bags which would then be taken by boat, to their rental car, and on to the local dump. "Donald at the dump was the first person in the area that we knew by name," Michael laughs.

With limited facilities, lots of hard work and local wildlife wandering through the shell of a home at all hours, the couple was spurred on to finish quickly. By the time Michael retired in 2004 the couple was spending four to five months making the island home. "Slowly but surely the place began to take shape. Every summer we returned to tackle a new project," Michael says. Over 13 years later the projects continue with the most recent addition being an outdoor shower, for a quick rinse from a river swim, complete with artistically-framed copper pipe uprights and covered in climbing vines.

"We wanted to keep true to the 'Adirondack' style (an American 'mountain camp' style created in the Adirondack Mountains of upstate New York). This style focused on natural materials such as stone, native woods and handcrafted furnishings. We tried to imagine our nature-loving president,

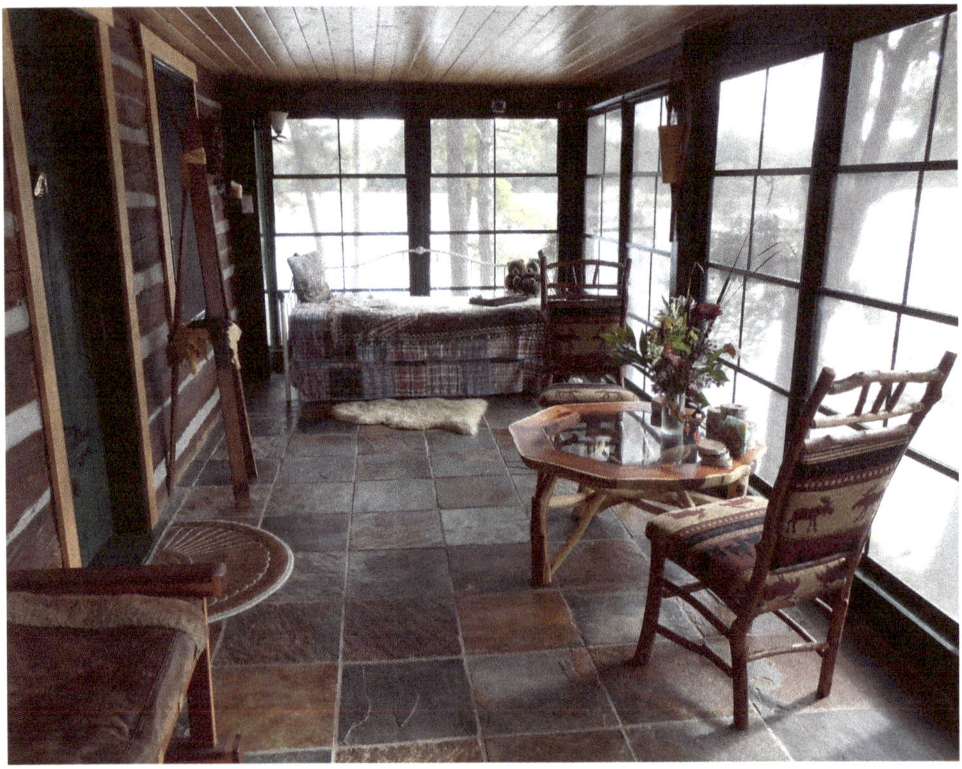

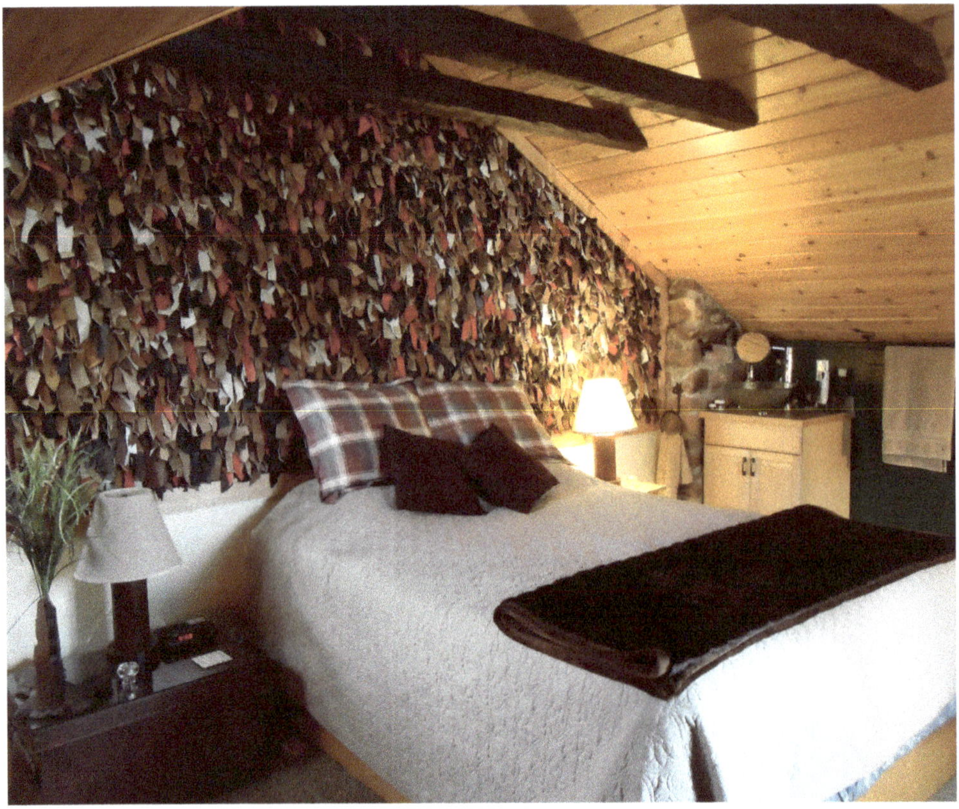

Teddy Roosevelt, and designer, Ralph Lauren, sitting on the dock smoking cigars and giving us the thumbs up! The hand-adzed cabin is over 135 years old and we accented the timber with hand-forged ironwork." That includes a Juliet balcony off the master bedroom and forged decorative hinges. Michael created these pieces at their village forge during their time in France.

"All the downstairs floors are slate and the massive granite fireplace in the living room was built with stones taken from our island's shore. This keeps us cosy on the shoulder season days when a bright fire is perfect on a cool river night."

Custom live edge wood furnishings are found throughout the home including a circular staircase made from a maple tree trunk with half rounds for steps and intertwining branches on the railing, a cherry wood burl dining table and, in the porch, a custom glass cocktail table revealing a base of twisted red cedar branches. Michael and Janice have also sourced Native Indian art and pieces such as the bespoke buckskin valances and drapes to truly keep with the style of the property.

"By focusing on the Adirondack style, we've kept the flow from indoors to outdoors seamless. All windows look out onto the water through our 84 pine, fir, cedar and oak trees. Blueberry bushes provide the groundcover. We chose to leave the island in its natural state without any formal landscaping and we've ensured with all our design choices that nature is the centre of our daily focus."

"People sometimes ask us if we have to use a boat to get out to the island. We tell them we don't *have* to use a boat…we *get* to use a boat! To us, there are no challenges, only opportunities. The Thousand Islands life on both sides of the river (Canada and USA) is geared to boaters with many restaurants, little theatres, a hospital, grocers, a hardware store and even a post office which all have little docks for easy access. We have island-wide Wi-Fi; satellite TV; reverse osmosis water purified from the tap; a washer; drier; dishwasher and trash compacter so life here is seamless and fairly challenge-free."

With five children and a growing number of grandchildren happy to visit Honey Bee Island each summer, it seems that Michael and Janice have truly found paradise. Michael, who is also a pilot, now has an amphibious floatplane docked at Honey Bee and admits that life really is pretty perfect. "Island life is just magical. It is a real 'pull-up-the-drawbridge' type of feeling as it's privacy without isolation. To look out any window of the house and see the river edged by forest in all directions…it doesn't get much better than this."

*You can learn more about this beautiful island home by visiting www.honeybeeisland.com - and find out more about Michael and Janice's other homes at www.vistaseas.com and www.villasurmer.com*

"People sometimes ask us if we have to use a boat to get out to the island. We tell them we don't have to use a boat...we get to use a boat!"

# Bruny Island, Australia
## Allegra & Adrian

The most southern state in Australia is Tasmania – or Tassie, as it's known to the locals. An island in its own right, Tasmania is separated from mainland Australia by the Bass Strait. In 1803 it became a penal settlement of the British Empire with approximately 75,000 convicts being sent to the state over a 50-year period. These days, the state is known for its magnificent produce (it's not just apples anymore: seafood, nuts, cheese, bread, honey, stone fruit, craft beer, whiskey and wines all find their way across the globe and are considered among the best). Wild and stunning scenery is another reason people flock to the region with white sandy beaches, craggy coastlines, wild rivers, hiking trails across picturesque mountain ranges and plenty of native wildlife.

Off the south-eastern coast of Tasmania lies Bruny Island. Technically two land masses (north and south, joined by a long and narrow sandy isthmus), Bruny Island has a total length of approximately 65 kilometres. Access to the island is by ferry from the mainland village of Kettering. The island was inhabited by Aborigines until European arrival in the late 1700s. In the late 1800s, the timber industry took off and Bruny Island was opened up by numerous tramways and haulages. Today, the island is known for its beautiful scenery and has been classified by BirdLife International as an Important Bird Area as it supports the world's largest population of the endangered forty-spotted pardalote, the critically endangered swift parrot and 12 of Tasmania's 14 endemic bird species.

Covering almost 1500 acres on South Bruny is a magnificent property called Labilliardiere Estate. Its two owners work hard to protect and maintain this beautiful part of the world, share their lives and educate others about life on Bruny Island.

Allegra and Adrian are an adventurous pair. Allegra is of British decent but was born and raised in Asia. After working as an educator of young children and as a health and fitness professional, she now owns and operates www.brunyislandexperience.com. She also manages to find time to work on her

artography (art photography) which you can find at www.allegrabiggsdale.com. Adrian is British and a retired marine engineer. Working with P&O until 1978, he then became a sought-after consultant in the oil and gas industry in Asia. Together, the couple have owned and operated a dive centre in the Maldives, sailed the high seas on their yacht '*l'aquila*', delivered yachts and climbed volcanoes!

It was their love of sailing that brought them to Bruny Island. "We were living in Jakarta and Adrian put together a campaign to sail a class vessel – a one tonner '*Beyond Thunderdome*' – in the 1990 Sydney to Hobart Race,'" Allegra explains. "Early January that year, we embarked on a road and ferry trip to Bruny Island after festivities had concluded, specifically to see the lighthouse at Cape Bruny Light Station." The lighthouse, first lit in 1838, is the second oldest in Australia and has the longest history (158 years) of being manned.

"Eight kilometres north of South Bruny National Park, I spotted a 'land for sale' sign on a tree," Allegra says. "I noted the number and on the way back we climbed the fence, took a walk to a wee cove and that was it for me. I made the phone call and within six months the purchase, though quite complicated, was complete. We returned that winter, eager to begin a new life on this island and to implement my vision of Labillardiere Estate – named after Jaques Labillardiere, ship's botanist and physician, on the scientific expedition in search of La Perouse, with French Admiral, Bruni D'Entrecasteux in 1792."

The island was actually named after this French explorer who searched the channel region and, by error in navigation, discovered it to be an island. It was known as Bruni Island until 1918 when the spelling was changed.

Allegra and Adrian have truly fallen in love with Australia, and their life on Bruny Island. "Australia is as diverse as it comes," Allegra says. "Its cultural mix makes it fascinating, despite its young history of just over 200 years. We love where we live…diverse natural values, birds, native flora and fauna, the coast, the five beaches we can access, amazing trees, clean air, mild winters, kind folk, artists across the genre…the list goes on!

"Mainland Australians joke that Tasmanians are 'two headed' and inbred from convict stock. Our perspective is: two heads are better than one," Allegra laughs. "Today, being of convict stock is actually

quite chic. For example, Nicholas Shakespeare, the reputed UK author, has written about his convict ancestry and makes Tasmania his home for at least half the year. Currently, mainlanders are selling up and migrating to Tasmania in droves for a multitude of reasons, not least its remarkable beauty. Tasmanians are the beneficiaries of new kids on the block — they bring change in their professional expertise, imagination, food and intellect, all contributing to an ever-increasing diverse state of discovery."

Allegra and Adrian have made use of their land to ensure that they have all they could need. They built a beautiful house that makes the most of coastal, mountain and natural vegetation views, as well as a guest cottage, overlooking Great Taylor's Bay, to accommodate local, national and international guests. An artists' studio, a beach hut on wheels, as well as a fabulous vegetable garden (covered to ensure that they aren't just feeding all of those birds!) is shared with guests. Long walking tracks meander throughout the property leading to magical coves and perfect places to relax and engage with nature and wildlife.

"We live in a very large aviary, so to speak. Our home has windows all around and although we have an eclectic mix of things, the lightness in colour and furniture still keeps it modern," Allegra says. The natural timbers and calm, light colours in the space set off the beauty beyond the windows. With a meditation room and lots of little places dotted around the house to sit and enjoy a cup of tea and a bird's song, it's any wonder Allegra and Adrian would never want to leave.

Despite their passion for Bruny Island, the couple have not lost their love for sea adventure. "Adrian loves the water, boats, tinkering with his Seagull Engine Collection and planning challenging adventures. His last was a circumnavigation in a 12-foot Huon pine clinker dinghy around Bruny Island using a silver century. The trip took 16 hours, in sometimes four-metre waves in our Southern Ocean.

This year he had hoped to complete a 300 mile UK Canal Classic with *'Frances'* his wooden dinghy currently stored in Suffolk."

The pair also continue to seek out places that offer them the opportunity to learn about nature different to that of Bruny Island. Their love of learning and adventure is certainly something that continues to keep them young. "In the last few years we've travelled for 30 days to the Sub Antarctic Islands and the Ross Sea in Antarctica and a month on a road trip through Rwanda and Uganda in Africa to climb in search of mountain gorillas, mingle with big game and extraordinary birds. Last winter we spent 15 days on a vessel and engaged with Darwin's finches and the fascinating land, air and marine fauna of the Galapagos Islands, then on to the Amazon – particularly for the birds – and high country in Ecuador for walking, volcanoes, flora and fauna."

*Discover more about Adrian and Allegra and their fabulous life by visiting www.brunyislandexperience.com or www.facebook.com/brunyislandexperience*

*"Tasmanians are the beneficiaries of new kids on the block — they bring change in their professional expertise, imagination, food and intellect, all contributing to an ever increasing diverse state of discovery."*

# Mahé, Seychelles
## Rachel, Unels, Tama & Shea

Seychelles – officially The Republic of Seychelles – is a 116-island country located northeast of Madagascar and about 1,600 km east of Kenya. The islands are made of what's considered to be the oldest and hardest granite in the world. The majority of the islands are uninhabited and many are dedicated as nature reserves. With just over 90,000 residents, Seychelles has the smallest population of any of the independent African states. Throughout most of recorded history, the Seychelles was largely unpopulated. First discovered by Portuguese sailors in the 1500s, the islands were used as a transit point between Asia and Africa and occasionally used by pirates until the French took control in the 1750s. Independence was established in 1976 as a republic within the Commonwealth and around this time the islands took off as 'the' place for film stars and the jet set to vacation.

The islands are known worldwide for their powedery-soft beaches and warm, turquoise waters. In fact, you are likely to find a Seychelles beach on most 'Top 10 Beaches' lists from around the globe – particularly the island of La Digue, with its giant, smooth granite rocks scattered around the shoreline. The largest island in Seychelles is Mahé, home to the country's capital, Victoria, and 86 per cent of the population. With just a 20-minute drive from the mountainous jungle in the centre of the island to one of the many pristine beaches, it's no wonder this place is viewed as paradise.

New Zealand-born Rachel left her hometown for a work and travel adventure 20 years ago and, at the time, Seychelles wasn't at all on her radar. "Rats had found their way on to Fregate Island, a place where they were particularly unwelcome as the island was a refuge for many of Seychelles endemic threatened species because it was totally rat-free. Being a Kiwi conservation practitioner, I had rat eradication experience," Rachel explains. "I was invited to Seychelles to get rid of the rats and I met Unels (who was working as a conservation biologist) – 18 years later and I am still here! We left briefly to live in the UK when I completed my PhD, but otherwise Seychelles has been home."

Rachel and Unels' two teenage children, Tama and Shea, were born in Seychelles and – like most teenagers – they love watching movies, playing sport and spending time with their friends. "They've both just taken up surfing and can last about five seconds standing on the board before falling off!" Rachel laughs. "There are lots of things we love to do as a family. Hiking, fishing and going to the beach to swim, snorkel and picnic."

Rachel and her family had been living on a smaller island in Seychelles – La Digue – for around three years before returning to Mahé to live and work. "We had nowhere to live," Rachel admits. "We rented a complete shack as it was affordable and then Unels cleared a piece of bush up on the mountainside and we built our own shack from recycled and second-hand wood and corrugated iron. We wanted a simple house that opened right across the front allowing for the great view and also for the ventilation. Seychelles is tropical, just four degrees south of the equator, so homes here don't need to be insulated. All a house needs to be is somewhere to keep the rain off – which this place does, after the few repairs undertaken during the first big downpour we had living here.

"We had no water inside the house for several months – just an alkathene pipe to bring water from a seep further up the mountain into a barrel outside the house. We used this to bathe and wash dishes and clean clothes until Unels added a bathroom and kitchen to the home. We also had no electricity for two years which, apart from our lovely, fully automatic white elephant of a washing machine sitting uselessly in the corner, was actually really great. We had plenty of energy as we went to bed in good time; Tama and Shea didn't get hooked on electronic gadgets and we read a lot of books by candlelight. Apart from electricity and the gadgets that come with it, the house hasn't changed a lot since then.

"A few years ago, we did convert half the verandah into a bedroom for Tama so that he and Shea could have their own rooms. Unels has built retaining walls so we have a bit of a flat lawn, and he is currently making us a big deck out the front of the house. Once it has a roof, we will be able to put a dining table, chairs and our sofa and coffee table out there – so then we will basically be able to live on the verandah. We also have a big vegetable garden, lots of fruit trees, chickens (for eggs and manure for the garden), tortoises (manure for the garden, and just because they are cool), guinea pigs (of no practical use but we love them!), a cat and a dog."

Rachel is quick to admit that most of the things in their home are practical rather than attractive and décor is not something that is given much thought. "We do like good quality, natural wooden furniture and materials though, and we are quite happy for things to be recycled or repurposed. Perhaps we could do with a few more cupboards to stow away the clutter."

For this outdoor-loving family, life couldn't get much better. "We do love our home. We have a really stunning view of the beach, the sea and neighbouring Silhouette and North Islands. We also have lots of green space around us; it's quite tranquil and agricultural which we love. It's also only five minutes to get to the beach for a swim!"

Rachel says that island life has its challenges, but they are things that you learn to adapt to. "Sometimes something that you want isn't available locally – which is perfectly understandable given Seychelles is isolated in the middle of the western Indian Ocean and the entire nation consists of only 90,000 people! It doesn't bother us too much, however anyone who is headed overseas always has a long shopping list to take with them. Even with the odd trip abroad, we've not accumulated much on our travels. When we lived in the UK we really only purchased warmer clothes. At the time we were living off our savings, so there was no money for 'things' as such. We also didn't want to ship anything back to Seychelles, so if it didn't fit in our suitcase on the way back home, it didn't make it back here! It is definitely easier to live a simpler life in Seychelles."

Another challenge that Rachel has found is ensuring that children raised in a tiny society such as Seychelles gets a bigger picture of the world. "We get around this by making sure we travel to other countries as much as our budget allows. We love to travel, but travelling is quite expensive from a small rock in the middle of the ocean, so we don't get overseas as much as we'd like. Mostly, we travel for work (UK and east African countries) and if budget allows we visit family in New Zealand. Otherwise, we go to La Digue for a holiday."

Like life anywhere, Rachel explains that you can often get caught up in the day-to-day. "A popular misconception is that life must be one long holiday when you live in a small island paradise. This, of course, isn't true. When you live and work here, as opposed to visiting on holiday, life can get too busy…just the same as everywhere else in the world!

"We are fairly adaptable and think we could live in most places, but for now we've no plans to go anywhere else – at least not until Tama and Shea finish school. You never know what the future holds. For now, we are happy, busy and settled here so may stay for good. Seychelles is visually stunning, warm and tropical. Being a small island nation, you're never too far from the beach or the mountains so it's a lovely place if you enjoy the outdoors. For us, right now, it's just perfect."

"We wanted a simple house that opened right across the front allowing for the great view, and also for the ventilation."

# Oki Islands, Japan
## Saki

Japan itself is an island country located in the Pacific Ocean in East Asia. A stratovolcanic archipelago of 6,852 islands, Japan has a population of 126 million – the world's 10th most populous nation. Japan is broken up into 47 prefectures, or regions, and the Oki Islands are part of the Shimane Prefecture to the west of the country. The Oki Islands have a total area of 346.1 square kilometres and only four of the 16 named islands are inhabited. Due to their geological heritage, the Oki Islands were designated a UNESCO Global Geopark in September 2014.

Dōgo is the largest of the Oki Islands. Roughly circular, it has an approximate diameter of 20 kilometres however with its highest point (the summit of Mount Daimanji) at 608 metres, it can be a scenic yet time-consuming drive when travelling from the port in the south up to the north of the island. The main town in Dōgo is Okinoshima. In 2004 all of the main villages of the island merged, so now the town technically occupies the entire island. With an estimated population of 14,850 the town (and island) is remote enough that it was once used as a place of political exile. Today, with a slow place of life, beautiful scenery (including giant cedar trees that are over 2,000 years old) and incredible diving and fishing available in the local beaches, it is a magical place that is well worth the journey.

A two-and-a-half-hour ferry ride across the Sea of Japan, followed by a 45-minute car journey to the very north of Dōgo is not the place you would expect to find a young Japanese web creator and a whole bunch of enthusiastic foreigners! However, for the last two years, *Tsukadaya*, a 120-year-old

traditional Japanese house, has been home to Saki, who now says that she simply cannot imagine living anywhere else. "I moved to this island two years ago from Shizuoka Prefecture," Saki explains. "As well as Shizuoka, I have lived in Tokyo, Sydney (Australia) and Fukuoka. I have lived in and visited many places but, for me, when I came to the Oki Islands, it was the first time that I just wanted to live in one place.

"When I first came here, I was just planning to stay on the island for two months. I really liked the lifestyle, the people, the nature and so I decided to live here. After that, many people helped me try and find a home and finally I met this old and gorgeous house."

This 'old and gorgeous house' is *Tsukadaya*. Once the home of a village leader it was, at one time, considered a mansion. Prior to Saki moving in, the house had lay empty for over 40 years. Saki was keen to convert the home into a guest house, but in doing so, she made very few changes. Other than slightly updating the kitchen and adding modern conveniences like running water and an indoor bathroom, the large home is just as it as has been for over a century. Guests stay on tatami floors in Japanese-style rooms and sleep on futons to enjoy the traditional feel.

"The house is on the north side of the island and it's just a five-minute walk to the beach," Saki says. "It's a location that you can spend a very peaceful time in. This home is huge and old Japanese style. Even on the hot summer days we are able to stay cool without a cooling device. It's lovely and calm and the perfect place to read books and just doze off."

Mind you, during the summer Saki has little time to relax with a good book. Sharing her love of the outdoors, local cuisine and the island itself with travellers from all over the world, Saki has become so busy that she has had someone move in with her to help over the high season. "I have someone come and live with me over the summertime to help with the workload. She is from Hyogo Prefecture and lives here for three months during the busier period."

Saki wanted to show other people exactly why she fell in love with the island and why she took the leap from the city to one of Japan's more remote areas. "We love fishing, diving to catch fish, riding our bicycles, climbing the mountains, growing vegetables, cooking…but mostly eating and drinking!" she says about the day-to-day activities.

Food is a big part of the experience at Tsukudaya and although guests can use the kitchen in the house at their leisure, Saki also offers those who are interested the chance to source food from the back garden and the ocean and then learn to cook it in traditional Oki Islands-style.

Saki says she just adores island life. Offering her guests fishing excursions or kayaking adventures through Dōgo's many sea caves is the perfect opportunity to explore her surroundings more each day. "There is so much to love about the Oki Islands. I love the lifestyle – being able to live with nature and enjoy all four seasons. The warmest and funniest people live here too. Unfortunately, the population of this island decreases year by year. I want to let many people love this island and I love to bolster the spirits of people living here."

Saki admits that many stereotypes about Japan may well be true, but they aren't negative. "Japan is small and clean with delicious food. The people are polite. We enjoy four beautiful seasons and there is such a unique history here," she says. "In the Oki Islands the people are even more lovely and friendly and it is so very beautiful here."

Despite her love of travel, Saki admits that she struggles to imagine herself anywhere else in the world. "I don't think I could ever live anywhere after finding my home here. I still do love to travel though – especially to other islands. I'd love to go to Okinawa and to Bali. I like the idea of going to places that are unexplored and not known to many other people."

*To have the opportunity to stay in Saki's guesthouse and explore all the Oki Islands has to offer, head to www.oki-tsukudaya.com*

"There's so much to love about the Oki Islands. I love the lifestyle - being able to live with nature and enjoy all four seasons. The warmest & funniest people live here too."

# Menorca, Spain
## Glòria & Miquel

The Kingdom of Spain is a sovereign state in southwestern Europe. The fourth largest European country by size and sixth largest by population, Spain's territory also include two archipelagos – the Balearic Islands in the Mediterranean to the east of the mainland, and the Canary Islands in the Atlantic Ocean off the African coast to the south. The four largest islands in the Balearic are Mallorca (also known as Marjorca), Ibiza, Formentera and Menorca (also known as Minorca).

Menorca has a population of just under 95,000. With a past that has seen the island occupied by Ancient Greeks, Romans, Turks, the British and the French, it offers an abundance of history. In 1993 Unesco declared Menorca a Biosphere Reserve not just to preserve its environmental areas, such as the Parc Natural S'Albufera d'es Grau wetlands, but also its many mysterious Bronze Age sites. With 216 km of glorious white, sandy coastline surrounding the island, and an estimated 70,000 km of dry stone walls criss-crossing through the fields and rolling hills, Menorca is as pretty as it is relaxed. Despite its reputation as the quiet neighbour (compared to Mallorca and Ibiza), Menorca still enjoys a fiesta and many of the popular festivals held throughout summer date back to the early 14th century.

Glòria and her husband, Miquel, fell in love with the Spanish island of Menorca over 30 years ago. Glòria, who spends much of her time working in Barcelona as a busy publicist in the art world, found the calm and relaxing island won her over from the very first moment. "I first came here in September, 1977," Glòria recalls. "A colleague invited me to her husband's birthday on Menorca. We arrived late

at night, drove straight from the airport to the coast and, as we were tired, we went straight to sleep. In the morning I went outside and..oh! I could not believe it. Cala Pregonda was the most beautiful beach I had ever seen. Certainly the most beautiful in Menorca, but perhaps even the most beautiful in the Mediterranean. It was the cover of Mike Oldfield's *Incantations* album come to life," Glòria laughs at the memory.

"The next year I went back several times and on one visit I went to the Fiestas de San Juan en Ciutadella (the Festival of Saint Joan of Ciutadella) which is one of the oldest festivals in Spain. That same visit I met Miquel. He had been going to the fiesta every year since doing military service in the Mola (a military fortress on the island). We fell in love with each other, and with Menorca."

Their love was cemented with an island wedding. "When our daughter, Rita, was seven years old we decided to get married. We had our wedding in Sant Lluís, which is a beautiful, authentic Menorcan town. It was the first time the Justice of the Peace had ever officiated a marriage and it was great fun."

In 1990, after vacationing over the years in various parts of the island, the couple decided to find a place of their own. "We bought a small apartment in the most emblematic place, Binibeca, which appears in all the guides and encourages tourists to visit. It's not an authentic fishing village, but it feels like one."

Glòria has decorated the home in a simple style to compliment the white washed walls and timber accents. "The apartment is in a development that was built in 1965 simulating a typical fisherman's house. It's small, but we make that 28-square metres go far! A living room, a fireplace, a little kitchen, two bedrooms, a bathroom, a small terrace and two balconies. The best part is that it is right in front of the sea.

"Mallorca and Ibiza are quite chaotic compared to Menorca. Unlike the noise and partying of Ibiza or the busy streets with lots of tourists of Mallorca, Menorca is a quiet and relaxing island and most holidaymakers who stay here live in nearby Catalonia. Life in the fishing village is very quiet. There are lots of traditional old sailing boats and with these boats the sailing is silent. "

Glòria says the sea is a big part of island life. "Clear water, white sands, cliffs, solitary lighthouses and small islets with gulls, cormorants and hawks... We fish tuna and raones, which are a small pink fish, and the most precious in Menorca after lobster. We race our little boats and fish at night with a full moon. During the day we walk by the horse-riding track. It is a beautiful life."

These days, daughter Rita (who now lives in San Francisco) often visits with her husband and young daughter, and Glòria and Miquel love their home and their island just as much as they did all those years ago. "I spend as much time as I can in Menorca, but I do love to travel. I have visited five continents; hitchhiked around Europe; caravanned in New Zealand and travelled through Alaska."

"Menorca really is like home for us though," Glòria admits. "Every year we return to this island, spending time with old friends, eating boiled lobster soup – made with the typical sauce of tomato and onion – and bread toasted by the sun. It is wonderful, my dear Menorca."

*"Clear water, white sands, cliffs, solitary lighthouses and small islets with gulls, cormorants and hawks... we fish, we race our little boats, we walk... it's a beautiful life."*

# Waiheke, New Zealand
## Anna, Nick, Molly & Thomas

Just 17.7 km from Auckland (New Zealand's most populated city) is the pretty island of Waiheke. It is the second largest island in the Hauraki Gulf after Hamilton Island. Home to over 8,700 residents, just under 20 km from top to bottom and less than 10 kilometres across at its widest point, it is New Zealand's most densely-populated island.

Voted the fifth best destination in the world by Lonely Planet in 2016, and voted fourth best island in the world in the Condé Nast Best Islands in the World list, Waiheke boasts a warm, dry microclimate; emerald waters, rocky bays and glorious sandy beaches. The region is also known for its fabulous wine with over 30 boutique wineries on the island (many with fancy restaurants and wonderful tasting rooms). Quirky galleries and craft stores hint at the island's hippy past and for the nature-lovers there are walking trails through nature reserves and excellent kayaking. The island is easy to access via air or ferry and has, over the years, become a popular holiday destination for North Island New Zealanders.

Artist and sculptographer, Anna; her creative entrepreneur husband, Nick and their two small children, Molly and Thomas, were living in Auckland when they first discovered Waiheke. "We had friends living on the island who we would visit and stay with on a regular basis," Anna says. "Every visit when it came time to head back to Auckland city we would be sad. So, we decided to sell our suburban inner city home and move to live a rural beach life with a sea view!"

Anna says that she was keen to make changes to the little 1950s weatherboard home the moment they moved in, but it took around five years before they started work. The wait paid off – allowing

her to accumulate the perfect items to create a beautiful sand and sea vibe. As the home was quite small, it was important to Anna that she kept a feeling of calm throughout – even in the places where bright colours were happily introduced. The colours, and the textures, of the home were inspired by the surroundings. Driftwood hat racks; ocean-inspired wall colours; tropical fabrics and art from local artists decorated the walls, creating a beachy, relaxed vibe from the moment you stepped inside.

"Flow to the outside and positioning living spaces was something that I really wanted to get right," Anna explains. "The outside landscaping and large windows made the exterior a big contributor as to how the interior aesthetics flowed and felt. Then, use of colour and nautical weathered elements reflected the island environment."

The alterations to the home allowed Anna and her family to fully embrace island life. "We lived a very relaxed, casual lifestyle. With two small children the open plan living, view to the garden, deck and patio were essential. The décor emulated our need to not be too precious and provided casual but beautiful aesthetics along with functionality. We wanted room for the kids to spread their numerous paraphernalia out (and be packed away, out of sight, in the blink of an eye). The wonderful window seat along the length of the large window that my clever husband built came in very handy! The décor also provided a place for us to entertain several kids play dates as well as grown up gatherings."

Anna and Nick's travels over the years have resulted in many great finds that looked perfectly at home in the Waiheke beach environment – like a Vietnamese rooster catcher cleverly used as a pendant light above the dining table, or the fabulous wire flower chairs on the deck that were found at Camden Markets in London.

Anna and Nick have recently taken advantage of new experiences and left the island...heading to an environment that is almost the antithesis of island life – Toronto, Canada! "My husband had a work opportunity and, being the adventurous characters that we are, we were up for the challenge," Anna laughs. "Although we miss family and friends incredibly – especially as the children are still so young – we have found ourselves loving and embracing the big city vibe. Toronto is a very easy and accessible city and it helps we've moved to an area that over 50 per cent of the population is made up of non-Canadian or non-Toronto natives. We love it for the cultural diversity it offers.

"We are also loving being able to explore not just our new land but also the countries nearby. Once a month we escape the city and explore a new area each time – Quebec, Montreal, Mexico and New York. Oh yes, New York! It's only a one and a half hour flight from Toronto and at any given opportunity, I am there in a heartbeat."

Despite the family's exciting new city life, Anna says that Waiheke is somewhere that she will always love. "It really is a beautiful island. Within a small distance there is such diversity in landscape. You can be surfing one day, skiing the next! Kiwis are a passionate and innovative lot with a relaxed and humorous outlook. It's an easy place to live in some respects, but the small population and isolation from the rest of the world does have its challenges.

"The commute was a 35-minute boat ride to downtown Auckland. We had a car downtown as well as an island vehicle. The boat ride was a welcome change… prior to our move we would find ourselves stuck in traffic on the motorway more often than not! The only restrictions were coordinating with the ferry timetable, which left on the hour – miss that scheduled sailing and you'd be stuck waiting for the next one. However, due to the popularity of the island and the visitor demand, you will now find ferries leaving every 15 minutes to half an hour, so waiting for the next boat isn't even an issue anymore!

"Waiheke has a passionate community – friends, beautiful beaches (frequented by us almost every single day of the year when we were there!), vineyards and an aspect of rural life. Whether we make it back to live there someday, or not, it will always have a very special place in our hearts."

*See more of Anna's gorgeous work, including her fabulous Sculptography limited edition fine art prints, at www.annachurchart.com*

*"Within such a small distance there is such diversity in landscape. You can be surfing one day, skiing the next!"*

# Bali, Indonesia
## Saffron, Simon, Chloe & Ginger

Bali is a contradiction known throughout the world for many reasons: a holiday destination and a retreat; a place to shop and party and a place where you can relax; somewhere you can find lively bars and top restaurants, as well as forested volcanic mountains, iconic rice paddies and beautiful beaches and coral reefs. Bali is at the westernmost end of Indonesia and includes a number of smaller islands such as Nusa Penida, Nusa Lembongan and Nusa Cenigan. With a population of just under four and a half million, Bali is home to Indonesia's Hindu minority. According to a recent census, 83.5 per cent of Bali's population follows Balinese Hinduism (followed by 13.5 per cent Muslim, 2.5 per cent Christianity and just 0.5 per cent Buddhism).

Bali has been inhabited since approximately 2000 BC and these peaceful people have experienced a number of battles in their history – from the Dutch invading in the 1800s and 1900s through to the war between the communists and the nationalists in the 1960s and, more recently, bombings by militant Islamists. Despite this, approximately 80 per cent of Bali's economy is driven by tourism. With warm tropical waters, stunning scenery and friendly locals, it's no wonder this part of the world is such a draw card to so many.

For the past 14 years, this Australian family has called Bali home and, given how embedded their careers are into the local culture, it doesn't seem like they will be saying farewell to this magical island any time soon. Saffron, who runs a clothing company, and Simon, a chef, have raised their daughters, Chloe (Coco) and Ginger, in this island paradise. Their current home is filled with all the colour and life you could hope for.

"We moved into this house seven years ago," Saffron explains. "Previously, we had lived on the coast in Petitenget, so it was a pleasant change to be amongst the rice paddies and the countryside. Our Balinese landlord had built the bones of a promising home and when we moved in, we installed everything – hot water, fans, the kitchen sink. We had grand plans to re-tile the bathrooms and put in a swimming pool, but that hasn't happened yet. We have painted the interior white though, which has made a big difference, but other than these small adjustments we haven't changed much.

"Despite many people moving in and building villas in our neighbourhood, I love our bumpy, one-car-wide road. Our home has a decent sized garden and the rooms are spacious. We get a delicious breeze, which makes a difference during the sticky wet season. Coco and Ginger can walk across the rice paddies to their school, which is a gift when they sleep late, and most days, all you can hear from our house is the rhythmic clacking of the bamboo wind catcher to stop the birds stealing rice from the fields."

Due to the warm and humid climate Saffron was keen to have a home that didn't rely on air conditioners to maintain a pleasant temperature, and it was this factor that won her over when choosing this house as home. "The first thing I noticed about this place was the cooling breeze. It felt like someone had switched on the air conditioner. We have planted a green lush garden with coconut and cempaka trees that aid in keeping the house cool and allow us to just rely on ceiling fans during the day. The house is open and airy and the white interior – including white floor tiles – is the perfect backdrop for my colourful and crowded design aesthetic."

Saffron isn't kidding when she says she loves colour. Growing up in a family of artists, her love of creativity is clear. "My father and my sister are ceramicists," she says. "My mother and my other sister are both painters. So, we are lucky to have a large and beautiful collection of art. We are also surrounded by photos of our family, and artwork created by the children. I collect folk art and textiles and our home is bursting with interior plants, orchids and flowers."

The other beautiful pops of colour found in every room are the stunning textiles. Saffron's clothing company, named *Coco & Ginger* after her girls, produces handmade, original designs on a small scale. "We work with family-owned and run tailors and home industry collectives of women to create our own designed fabrics and hand-stitched embroideries. We have a fair pay and living wage policy and many of the textiles in our home are from our collections over the years."

Saffron has truly embraced life in Bali during her time living there, even with its many quirks. "We love being part of a vibrant Hindu culture. This past week has been Nyepi and the entire island shuts down — including the airport and roads. People stay inside their homes for 24 hours for silent meditation and TV is not watched and meals are not cooked. This year it coincided with an almost full eclipse in the morning, which was incredible to see. Then, in the evening, the stars blew us away. The night before the silence we watched the incredible parades of Ogoh-Ogoh demons, which are giant paper maché monsters carried through the streets on bamboo platforms. During this celebration, the sound of Gamelan was echoed through the hills. It's wonderful."

She does admit though, that Bali life does sometimes has its challenges. "Island fever is sometimes an issue and takes time to reboot. A quick trip to Singapore normally cures me and, after a few days, I am ready for the earthy smells and chaotic traffic of Bali. I do struggle with the traffic. I've always driven and, over the years, the number of cars has increased so much. Some days it feels like you're stuck in an episode of *Top Gear*!"

Crazy traffic aside, Saffron says that, for now at least, Bali is well and truly home. "We are not Balinese, so I am sure we will eventually live somewhere else. I hope to always have somewhere to call home on this beautiful island though, and I know I will have my Balinese friends forever. We went to Paris for a holiday recently and it was incredible. We've become passionate Francophiles and often dream of the apartment that we'd have there. Coco hopes to spend some time studying there when she's older.

"One thing is for sure though…Bali will always be in our hearts forever. This island has welcomed us with smiling lips and sparkling eyes for these past years — and hopefully for many more years to come."

*Get inspired by more of Saffron's colourful art and designs by visiting her website: www.cocoandginger.com*

"Most days, all you can hear from our house is the rhythmic clacking of the bamboo wind catcher to stop the birds stealing rice from the fields."

# Phillip Island, Australia
## Ian & Madeleine

The Victorian coastline, in the south of the Australian mainland, is known for its magical beaches and stunning scenery. Often the Great Ocean Road to the west of the state's capital, Melbourne, is the region that receives the most press. However, to the east of the state, the coastline is just as pretty as you travel from the Mornington Peninsula to Gippsland. The Bass Coast Shire is situated in the centre and with a population of just under 30,000 throughout an area of 864 kilometres, it's no wonder that much of the region is untouched and full of natural beauty.

A 640 metre bridge connects the town of San Remo in the Shire to the island town of Newhaven, on the 100-kilometre square Phillip Island. The island was occupied by British settlers in 1842 and the bridge, linking the island to the mainland, was originally wooden and was built over two years from 1938. Famous for its wildlife, Phillip Island is home to significant populations of fairy penguins, short-tailed shearwaters and Pacific gulls. At the wildlife park wallabies and kangaroos can be fed by hand and at Seal Rocks, on the west of the island, you will find the largest colony of fur seals in Australia. In recent years, Burranan dolphins, killer whales, southern right whales and humpback whales have started to show increased numbers in the area. Tourism is a big part of the economy and 3.5 million people visit the island annually. Various surf events have been held on the island and since 1928 international races have run on the Grand Prix Circuit, including those for motorbikes and, most recently, V8 supercars.

Ian and Madeleine are a couple with a passion for travel and the finer things in life. Both Australian-born, the pair have lived, worked and travelled their way around the globe. "We've lived and worked in Singapore, London, Philadelphia and Australia," says Ian. "We have travelled extensively

through Asia, the US and Europe over the last 40 years and we've also travelled a great deal around Australia. We lived on Groote Eylandt in the Gulf of Carpentaria for three years — back then it was even more remote than it is today — and we saw a lot of the remote parts of Australia in that time."

*Glen Isla House*, the couple's homestead on Phillip Island, has been in the family since 1982. "At the time, it was purchased by Madeleine's brother, as a beachside retreat," Ian explains. "The homestead dates back to 1870 and is on land that was part of one of the original grants in the 1800s. It is believed to have originally been on 300 acres of land, but over the years it was reduced to just one third of an acre. In 1999, Madeleine's brother retired to Queensland so we purchased the property from him with a view to create a boutique accommodation offering for discerning travellers. In 2003 we moved in and that same year we opened the property for guests.

"Over the years we have purchased additional properties around the original homestead, so *Glen Isla House* now encompasses just under two acres, on six different land titles — all of which were part of the original property. The additional properties had mature trees including three oaks that are over 100 years old, and five Norfolk pines that are around the same age. They provide a beautiful canvas to recreate the lovely private heritage garden the homestead is nestled in."

When Ian and Madeleine purchased the property, they set about restoring it to its former glory. "We constructed some additional buildings including purpose-designed guest accommodation, a self-cater cottage, a garage, an office and a purpose-built wine cellar, all of which blends architecturally into the grounds and historic homestead," Ian explains.

The result of all their hard work is a stunning home and nine rooms of guest accommodation rented to short-stay visitors from all over the world. "We've always had a love and appreciation of history, old homes and classic, elegant style," says Ian, who is also a trained chef and prepares a special breakfast for his guests when they stay. "The main residence is furnished with genuine antiques and Persian rugs creating an elegant ambience in the historic home. We are keen members of the National Trust and have hosted National Trust visits to *Glen Isla*. The extensive and private heritage gardens offer a buffer to the surrounding residential area and also a serene and peaceful environment for us to live in. Guests who come and stay with us love this aspect of the property...not to mention that just

120 metres from the back door we have direct access to a beautiful beach."

Given that *Glen Isla House* has been in the family for many years, Ian says that it has become a second home for extended family. "Our children are adults now and they grew up celebrating Christmas and summer here. Now their children, our grandchildren, are growing up with holidays at the homestead. *Glen Isla* has provided many fond memories for us. Ultimately, we will probably move to Melbourne to be closer to them and closer to medical facilities when we get older, but it will be a sad day when we do leave Phillip Island.

"Melbourne is just two hours away so perfect for retail therapy or a theatre 'escape' but Phillip Island is a wonderful place to live. It's an island lifestyle, a beach lifestyle and a country lifestyle all rolled into one! The permanent population of the island is around 4,500 and this swells over the summer holidays to something like 40,000. For the most part though, the township of Cowes – where we are – is a small country town, set by a north-facing beach. There are pristine sandy beaches; spectacular surf beaches; wetlands with extensive birdlife; wildlife experiences including the little penguins, fur seals and koalas and yet there are also world-class restaurants, a multi-award winning winery and the Phillip Island Grand Prix Circuit.

"Because the island is 'drive-on and drive-off' thanks to the bridge, we are not isolated when it comes to supplies. However, it can be challenging when you need a spare part or a serviceman to repair a piece of equipment! You have to be a bit of a handyman yourself. Perhaps the greatest challenge of the island is the fact that there is no hospital and the nearest emergency room is almost an hours drive away. The air-ambulance does service the island though and we have an excellent medical centre."

Ian and Madeleine operate *Glen Isla* from September through April every year and close for guests over winter. "This allows us to undertake annual maintenance on the property, give everything a good deep clean and take a well-earned break from the business," Ian says. "Most years we take our four-wheel drive and off-road camper trailer and try and see some of the vast Australian outback. In 2013 we did a trip through the Tanami Desert to the Kimberley region in northwest Australia and then

travelled across to Broome and Cape Leveque. Last year we followed part of the old Ghan railway and visited parts of the Simpson Desert. Every two to three years we try to get to Europe.

"As a chef, my favourite destination would have to be France. We've been there many times and there is a great deal there to excite my food passions! Madeleine has a passion for history, so she is very satisfied in France also, with visits to chateaus and cathedrals. We do love Italy, England and Germany as well.

"We feel very fortunate that we have a life that enables us to taste the best of both worlds – overseas destinations and life in Australia. There really is no place like home though. Australia offers so much in terms of lifestyle, with a stable political system and rule of law. With the right attitude, anyone can get on and be successful in this country. We've lived in other countries, so we have some experiences to compare with. We have thoroughly enjoyed our time in these locations, but there really is no place like Australia."

*To see more of the historic and beautiful Glen Isla House, visit www.glenisla.com*

"Our children are adults now and they grew up celebrating Christmas and summer here. Now their children, our grandchildren, are growing up with holidays at the homestead."

# Photo Credits

Cover image: (Fofoa Island, Tonga) **Karyn von Engelbrechten**

Page 3: (Streymoy, Faore Islands) **Mauritia Kirchner**

Pages 4 & 5: (Watercolour World Map) **Pavlo Raievskyi**

Page 6: (Harbour Island, Bahamas) **Sarah Wood**

Page 7: (Djerba Island, Tunisia) **Belinda Grootveld**

Pages 8, 9, 10, 11, 12, 13, 14, 15: (Fofoa Island, Tonga) **Karyn von Engelbrechten**

Pages 16, 17, 18, 19, 20, 21, 22, 23: (Streymoy, Faore Islands) **Mauritia Kirchner**

Pages 24, 25, 26, 27, 28, 29, 30, 31: (Harbour Island, Bahamas) **Sarah Wood**

Pages 32, 33, 34, 35, 36, 37, 38, 39: (Djerba Island, Tunisia) **Belinda Grootveld**

Page 40: (Mary image - Isle of Skye, Scotland) **Mary Arnold-Foster**

Pages 41, 42, 43, 44, 45: (Isle of Skye, Scotland) **Huntley Hedworth**

Page 46: (Claire image - Lesvos, Greece) **Carla Coulson**

Pages 47, 48, 49, 51, 52, 53: (Lesvos, Greece): **Claire Lloyd**

Pages 54, 55, 56, 57 58, 59, 60, 61: (Rarotonga, Cook Islands) **Susanna Wigmore**

Page 61: (Top image - Rarotonga, Cook Islands) **Eric Gamez**

Pages 62, 63, 64, 65, 66, 67, 68, 69: (Honey Bee Island, Canada) **Michael Laprade**

Page 70: (Bruny Island, Australia) **Richard Bennett**

Pages 71, 73, 74, 75, 77: (Yellow Tailed Black Cockato - Bruny Island, Australia) **Allegra Biggs Dale**

Pages 72, 76: (Settler's Way & Odyssey Studio - Bruny Island, Australia) **Jennifer Skabo**

Pages 76: (Vegetable Garden & Cockle Cove - Bruny Island, Australia) **Alice Hansen**

Page 77: (Superb Fairy Wren, Bottom image - Bruny Island, Australia) **Warwick Berry**

Pages 78, 79, 81, 82, 83, 84, 85: (Mahé, Seychelles) **Rachel Bristol**

Page 80: (Bottom image - Mahé, Seychelles) **Naomi Doak**

Pages 86, 87, 88, 89, 90, 91, 93: (Oki Islands, Japan) **Saki Furukawa**

Pages 94, 95, 96, 97, 98, 99, 100, 101: (Menorca, Spain) **Glòria Conesa**

Pages 102, 103, 104, 105, 106, 107, 108, 109: (Waiheke Island, New Zealand) **Kevin Emirali**

Pages 110, 111, 112, 113, 114, 115, 116, 117: (Bali, Indonesia) **Nikole Ramsay**

Pages, 118, 119, 120, 121, 122, 123, 124, 125: (Phillip Island, Australia) **Dave Temple for Glen Isla**

# Want more?

Visit our website to discover more titles and sign up so you are up-to-date with every new book on offer!

**www.oftheworldbooks.com**